ENDORSEMENTS FOR CONQUER YOUR YIPS, WIN THE EMPLOYMENT YOU TARGET

This is a thinking golfer's and non-golfer's approach to job search. Chuck likens the stress that leads to golfing "yips" to the stress that leads to career search "yips." He provides insightful, common-sense strategies for preparing, practicing and following a game plan to score the job you are looking for.

—Angela Foote
Old Greenwich, Connecticut

It has been said, sometimes to cliché, that the game of golf mirrors real life. With that thought in mind Mr. McConnell has written an excellent book that is no cliché! By making a comparison between the psychological and mental skill sets needed to play golf and the surprisingly similar "head" issues that one needs to address in a job search, he is spot on with "Conquer Your Yips: Win the Employment You Target." This read is informative while keeping the reader entertained with a little fun.

—Martin Berlin
American Airlines Retired Manager of Flight and
Chief Pilot New York; FAA Designee Check Pilot and Instructor;
USAF six year active duty Vet and Retired Reserve Maintenance
Quality Control Officer/Wing Test Pilot

I truly enjoyed the book. Lots of good stuff in here, actually, wish I read something like this way back when. Not your usual job search guide! A highly readable book based on the premise that preparing to win in golf, or any sport, is essentially the same as developing and executing a successful job search. Using a golf analogy, each chapter offers a compact summary of practical, proven ideas that will get results. Conquer Your Yips will unquestionably help you land that job you want, it might even improve your golf game.

—Peter Wilder
Retired, Business Development Director,
Pfizer Animal Health Division

Thoroughly enjoyed this book, and the comparisons between business careering and the game of golf. An ingenious comparison of career search challenges with the vicissitudes of golf. A great short read!

—Tom Healy, Retired Global Bank Relationships Manager,
Texaco Inc. Formerly Pan Am, Martin Marietta.
Corporate Finance.

Chuck presents a unique (and persuasively relatable) proposition to gain new employment. I learned a great deal and appreciate the metaphor and the advice. It applies not only for job interviews but also to equity and grant application submissions. The more choices you identify the better your confidence at winning the employment you seek.

—Ted Hoster, President,
Triumph Marketing Group, Centennial, Colorado

Every job-seeker needs this book! Packed with antidotes so you'll avoid those job-hunting whiffs, flubs and yips.

—Lucy Hedrick, publishing coach and author,
"Five Days To An Organized Life "

A fascinating book about the challenges most of us face in our working lives ... getting the new job. Whether the objective is a better position or returning to the work force, Chuck's analogies are based on his golfing observations. Chuck recommends confirming a grip on your objectives and concentrate with a laser eye on your target... all to get the best "lie" in the "rough" to make the best shot at new employment!!!

—Michael Smith; Retired Vice President, Elof Hansson Inc., a sub of Elof Hansson A.B, Gothenburg, Sweden, servicing the wood pulp, paper, waste paper, paper making machinery, timber industries

Author McConnell alerts the reader that his goal is simple: to provide assistance to an individual in his/her job search plan when the process has become bogged down, without signs of success. He uses the language and analogy of golf "yips", those strange and sudden appearances of mysterious afflictions that detract from a golfer's success on the golf course. The comparisons provide a fascinating platform to identify possible weaknesses in your job search presentation by relating them to amateurs' efforts on the golf course. He then makes corrective suggestions to strengthen the search program. Eminently readable, this book will provide valuable solutions to aspiring job seekers and career changers, and maybe some amateur golfers.

—Donald R. Kiefer, Esq., Attorney at Law

Dear Mike,
All good wishes!
Should you encounter 'Yips' I am confident
that they are quickly ‘Conquered’
Best regards
Chuck

CONQUER YOUR YIPS:

Win the Employment You Target

How Understanding Golf Stress
Defeats Job Search Stress

CHUCK
McCONNELL

ARCHWAY
PUBLISHING

Archway Publishing books may be ordered through booksellers or by contacting:

Archway Publishing
1663 Liberty Drive
Bloomington, IN 47403
www.archwaypublishing.com
1 (888) 242-5904

Because of the dynamic nature of the Internet, any web addresses or links contained in this book may have changed since publication and may no longer be valid. The views expressed in this work are solely those of the author and do not necessarily reflect the views of the publisher, and the publisher hereby disclaims any responsibility for them.

Any people depicted in stock imagery provided by Thinkstock are models, and such images are being used for illustrative purposes only. Certain stock imagery © Thinkstock.

Original Illustrations by Thomas Hilley

ISBN: 978-1-4808-1463-9 (sc)
ISBN: 978-1-4808-1464-6 (hc)
ISBN: 978-1-4808-1465-3 (e)

Library of Congress Control Number: 2015901863

Print information on the last page.

Archway Publishing rev. date: 03/30/2015

This book started as a concept some three years ago. It would not have gotten to this finished stage without the help and motivation I received from my superb support group:

My wife, Nancy, who helped me in so many ways as validator and sous-chef in getting the right ingredients together in a way that made sense.

My proofreader, Angela Foote, who helped make this effort readable and in a form that my English professor could read without cringing.

And my good friend, published author Lucy Hedrick, whose enthusiasm encouraged me to complete the project before it entered year four.

Contents

Preface

How Golf Experiences Can Help Your Job Search

C harles (Chuck) McConnell knows yips as unconscious responses caused by stress on the golf course. He describes and compares them to similar stress-related yips he has seen and helped correct for his clients who are searching for a new job or a career change. As an avid, though very amateur, golfer he presents actionable job-hunting suggestions that are easily understood by both golfers and non-golfers. In *Conquer Your Yips: Win the Employment You Target,* McConnell explains how yips plague job seekers when a stressful job search is underway. By comparing golfing stress issues to search stress issues, McConnell offers memorable, helpful analogies designed to improve results for all seeking new employment.

The challenges in golf are frustrating and not easily conquered. Preparing to win in career employment search is quite similar. As a career transition professional, Chuck says, "It is quite apparent every time I tee it up that the same counterproductive forces are at work in each endeavor." In golf, there are hazards aplenty along the way. Golf courses warn golfers by tagging their hazards with white, yellow, and red stakes. Knowing how to remediate golf hazards is covered by the USGA Rules of Golf. While often painful, golfers find formal rules helpful. Similar signs and answers are not present in search. It is up to the individual to learn to identify and, if possible, avoid potential problems. Career searchers need to think through the what-ifs that may be encountered during their new employment efforts. Planning and well-defined preparation are required to conquer the stress that Chuck refers to as "search yips."

The primary thesis developed in this book is that stress reactions existing in the game of golf are directly comparable to similar stress issues afflicting job searchers. In his professional practice Chuck has identified how search yips can strike and impede otherwise highly qualified job applicants. When stress is identified and minimized, employment search will focus on campaign preparation and candidates will be more productive. Creating a searcher's Unique Brand Equity (UBE) is the initial recommendation in *Conquer Your Yips, Win the Employment You Target*. McConnell presents methods to create that winning UBE for all those looking to qualify for new employment opportunities. Armed with this important competitive candidacy element, searchers will build confidence to conquer their yips.

For the past fifteen years, McConnell has assisted clients searching for new career paths. As past President/COO of Stewart, Cooper & Coon, the highly acclaimed career transition management firm with headquarters in Phoenix, Arizona, he has helped prepare many candidates for interviews and employment negotiating sessions. Presently, as Principal, Executive Managing Director of Stewart, Cooper & Coon-CT based in Stamford, CT, his proven insights continue to assist thousands of individuals in search.

Help has arrived for today's job seekers who choose to take dead aim at their new career targets to conquer the hazards and the annoying search yips in their way.

Chapter One
Introduction

Teeing Off

Do We Really Need Another Job Search Self-Help Book?

Maybe not—but this is not the traditional "How to Get a Job" search book. It is a compilation of practical, usable ideas and job-hunting solutions I have advocated for two decades with job searchers ranging from recent graduates to senior-level executives. As CEO of First Career and Find Career in the early nineties, then as President, COO of Stewart, Cooper & Coon, and today as Principal, Executive Managing Director of SCC-CT, I have helped develop and refine the insights and tactics that have helped many in successful career transition.

There are millions today, perhaps like you, who are actively searching for new and improved employment and becoming frustrated at every step. But searchers are not clamoring for another job-hunting book to add to the more than 50,000 career related titles in print today. In this book I present my central idea that stress in the job search process is quite similar to the stress most golfers experience. I compare those stresses to help searchers, golfers and non-golfers alike, gain new insights and perspective about the stresses they face in job campaigns. The fully employed, unemployed, and underemployed will benefit from comparing golf stress to what they are dealing with in the world of employment search.

In my practice at SCC-CT I meet with talented people each week who are engaged in frustrating, protracted career search. All have the requisite levels of formal education and have experienced excellent employment success within many diverse private, public, for-profit and not-for-profit organizations. Yet, despite intelligently constructed campaigns, interviews leading to their next employment opportunity are a scarce commodity due to today's negative economic condition and the large volume of competitors. In this book I present what we counsel our clients who are working to discover their next employment. I choose to express my suggestions in a conversational manner, inspired by *Harvey Penick's Little Red Book of Golf.* In writing *Conquer Your Yips, Win the Employment You Target,* I want to offer help wherever you are in your search. By flipping open to any chapter of your choice or by reading through in sequence, the suggestions offered in each chapter present campaign tactics proven to overcome stress and conquer employment search yips.

What's With the Title, "Yips?"

Yips is a term commonly used in golf. In other pursuits yips may be called tics, freezing, jerks, quirks or hiccups—but I think yips truly sums it up for both golfer and non-golfer. Historians report that Scottish golf legend Tommy Armour suffered from the yips. He defined the malady as "a brain spasm that impairs the short game." He stated that some of his chips and putts that ran amok were the direct result of his yips. Hank Haney, superb all-pro golf instructor, defines yips as an involuntary disruptive movement of the hand, wrists, and forearms that causes an otherwise predictably simple golf shot to perform in very strange and unintended ways. Hank confirms that yips deliver a disordered response leading to off-kilter, errant results on the course.

The golfer usually knows what is required to make a shot. Just address the ball and swing the club. Make contact with the ball and watch while it takes a perfect arc toward the flag on the green! But all too often some unexplainable action takes over, making the simplest chip or putt turn horribly wrong. As Competitive-Golfer.com suggests, "when you face a tough golf shot, stress (yips) can take over and cause you to lose control." Within nanoseconds your brain's neurons fire up, your adrenaline surges, your muscles tighten, and your breathing becomes faster and shallower. Adrenaline surges may be exciting in some contexts, but excitement quickly disappears when your shot fails to end up where you intend. Golfers know about the yips but the affliction may also crop up in a variety of ways and in many different pursuits. Musicians, writers, public speakers, and athletes in other sports also have suffered from the yips. Whenever they occur in a serious endeavor, they are definitely unwelcome.

Though far from a professional, I am an avid golfer. I love the game, despite my futile attempts to perfect it. While playing over the years and as a professional in executive placement, I have realized that the preparation needed for making a golf shot is quite comparable to the mental and physical preparation needed for a successful job search. In my opinion, when one is in search and up against multiple stresses involving ego, family, reputation, change of location, and financial issues, the situation is ripe for a yips attack. Searchers may think they know how to conquer employment pressures and present their candidacies in a positive light; but, under stress, involuntary responses or yips may take over to ruin the day. I have described a variety of golfing-related yips. Comparable ones may make an appearance in your search effort and become distractors, disruptors, and even destroyers of an otherwise perfectly planned job search. Perhaps you will see yourself in some of the scenarios. Summing up, yips are those unplanned and unhelpful responses to trying situations that impair coordination, mental strength, and confidence. Now that I have provided my definition of yips, can you see how understanding this affliction may be helpful in job search? I hope you are open to seeing why both understanding career search yips and conquering them are helpful, if not mandatory, to winning the employment you target.

My Goal in Writing Yips

My goal in writing this book is to change the perception of why your search may have failed to gain traction and provide my ideas for solutions. I believe the golf-to-search analogy, though unconventional, provides a fresh slant on the process. My focus is to show you how to overcome the hazards that occur in search and address the disappointment of repeated interview failures. Using the proven tactics presented in this book, your focus will improve as you take a new approach to increasing confidence and enthusiasm for the work ahead.

On a regular basis in my practice, yips become our focus as we prepare clients for interviews using intense simulated "grilling" sessions. As my professional career transitioning team and I prepare these clients for job interviews, we see clear signs of actual and potential yips. When the video of practice sessions is viewed, our clients can see the issues too. Bringing yips to their attention is useful, even if they are unable to conquer them immediately or totally. Just as in golf, viewing potential problems and becoming aware of possible fixes are useful to conquering them over time. This exercise, both unfamiliar and frightening to some, can lead to outstanding results at the interview table. The critical element here is an active desire to engage in honest introspection to build self-awareness spurred on by a dedication to reach the target employment. Throughout this book I provide my ideas about the current job search scene. Take a moment to review from your perspective the following general questions about job search.

1. How are the competitive realities of job hunting in the twenty-first century creating stress-producing challenges for your search?

2. How does effective coaching in golf compare to objective, professional job coaching for employment seekers?

3. How can those who have given up and dropped out of job search be reached and motivated to return with new solutions to reach their targets?

4. How will awareness of individual stress help one maintain a calm demeanor and positive focus in conquering yips?

5. How does working to conquer your yips translate into a strengthened employment search?

As you read, I encourage you to compare your current employment search direction, your line of attack, to my suggested approach. This will help you gain a new awareness of opportunities to focus and improve your search. I have presented techniques to limit, if not totally conquer, yips in your careering efforts. Our starting point will be establishing your individual brand identity, your unique value proposition that I call Unique Brand Equity (UBE). This becomes the foundation for winning the employment you target.

Let's tee off!

Chapter Two

Branding on the PGA Compared to Branding in Employment Search

Brand Aura

"Branding" is a classical consumer product management term. It refers to assuring that products, through positioning and marketing tactics, are competitive in the marketplace. Having created and developed brands for Fortune 500 marketers and their advertising agencies, I am certain that branding, if done well, positively differentiates a product or a service from others. Through unique presentation, packaging, pre-emption, trademarking, patent process, copyright protection, and user testimonials, a product can become a brand. Brand is an important topic in career coaching seminars these days, yet many still believe that they need only their resume, a chronological listing of who they are and what they have done, to succeed in search. That is certain to lead to failure. Additionally, job searchers with generic or anemic brands project a nondescript image and risk losing out to full-throated, well-branded competitors in the head-to-head employment battle. Failing to have an effective, compelling personal brand undermines your individual value, suggesting you might consider a lower level position or a below-market compensation package.

Professional golfers and the marketers of golf equipment obviously understand the value of branding, perhaps to excess. As logo-festooned professional golfers supported by lucrative endorsement fees step up to the tee, we know that, as fans of both the sport and the players, we are being targeted. The "branding game" as seen on television has become a colorful parade of embroidered logos on hats, shirts, shoes, golf bags, and equipment. As a marketing guy I especially appreciate the promotional value when audiences in the millions view the distinctive golf bags, clubs and ball logos displayed in ultra-close-ups at crucial moments during play. Those close-ups are worth millions! The golfers' identities—their personal brands—are being transferred to branded golf equipment as well as to other categories like energy drinks, dietary supplements, even technology and consulting firms. The logos and names of every brand known in the golfing world bask in the halo effect generated by the pro golfers who endorse, use, and wear them. That brand visibility on the televised PGA tour generates high value advertising for the companies involved, especially if the golfers are on the top of the leaderboard. Brand image creates consumer interest while it encourages product preference, new trial, and repeat purchase. Those mini-ad logos and endorsements create substantial wealth for the pros that occasionally exceeds the prize purses of the tournaments in which they play. It is tough to question that value is created by brand identity.

Looking at golf's history we can see the early start of personal branding for professional golfers too. Bobby Jones's classy demeanor and great play helped popularize the game in the 1920s. His name was Robert but he became known as Bobby. His brand name did not conflict with his contemporary, Robert Trent Jones, the famous course designer, known as Trent. Even decades ago it was obvious that branding should be differentiated to avoid confusion. In more recent times, Arnold Palmer, "The King" and his umbrella, still an everyman-brand sports hero, had many legendary head-to-head competitions with equally well-branded Jack Nicklaus, "The Golden Bear," and Gary Player, "The Man in Black." My personal favorite is Tom Watson, who continues to be competitive playing against pros half his age. His brand image, as resident pro at the famous Greenbrier Resort, includes his advice to play it forward, which encourages more seniors to play and have more fun by using up front tees.

Today's professional golfers have, maybe by accident, built their own personal brands through their distinctive appearance, personalities, and approaches to the game—for example, Jim Furyk's odd, though highly effective, "loop de loop" swing pattern or Craig Stadler's personality enhanced by his walrus handlebar stash. Sergio Garcia's youthful exuberance and immediate likeability allow his fans to forgive and forget his once tedious, repetitive waggles before each shot. Greg Norman's uber-Aussie headgear and his "shark" nickname support his no-fear, take-no-prisoners approach to the game. Matt Kuchar's wonderful smile and winning attitude are ever present despite very occasional setbacks from missed short putts. (Of course, his perennial top-ten pro ranking justifies his smile.) Phil Mickelson's devil-may-care course management and miracle recovery shots are regular crowd pleasers. "Lefty" is part of his brand and fans clamor for him to don another green jacket at Augusta. Ernie Els' "Big Easy" nickname is based upon his incomparably smooth swing that most every golfer would love to have.

Top-tier U.S. and international pros have helped bring the game to prominence today. It is the most popular individual sport in the world. Golf, scheduled to be played in the 2016 Olympic

Games, is interesting to a diverse universe of golfers and non-golfers alike. In many ways, I feel that televised golf was reality television before that genre was developed. One got to know the players and their struggles, see their wives and children, and appreciate their skills in super close-up shots. Its continuing popularity is based in large part on the human interest stories and the distinctive personalities (the brands) of the players.

Each of the gifted golf pros I have mentioned has, at one time or another, fallen victim to cases of the yips. Each found methods to conquer the yips through coaching, practice, and hard work. They have been my inspiration to compare golf yips to the wide variety of stressful obstacles that exist in employment search.

Branding to Win in Employment Competition

Today's competitive job market requires that candidates have brand differentiation because employers are selecting from large pools of talent fighting for the all-too-few career level opportunities. In the following chapters, I describe how you can learn to construct and use your unique brand that will make your candidacy stand out from the competition. I want you to think of your brand as your personal asset account containing the leadership and competencies you have earned throughout your career. It is your personal career brand equity and it is unique. I have termed it Unique Brand Equity (UBE). With your UBE positioning you will not be viewed as just another generic contender. You won't be left behind in the dust by higher-profile, branded, and distinctively presented candidates. It is risky to allow a potential employer to interpret your brand, your potential value to them, without providing your input. I see that unfortunate scenario unfold with many in search, especially those looking to change career fields, and our ex-military clients. Most veterans have established outstanding technical and leadership competencies serving our country; but, like other career-changing candidates, they can be pigeonholed and considered less appropriate or "too different." They need to establish their brand equity based on the transferability of their proven competencies. In all cases, presenting unique capabilities through your UBE will provide the competitive edge you require to build on your past successes and discover new career opportunities.

At this point, I trust you are realizing that it is critical to establish your personal branding strategy and forge a positive competitive position that you can own. By not presenting a unique, branded candidacy you may appear ill defined, unsupportable, and generally less than compelling as a candidate. Unlike pro golfers' endorsements that command attention, you can't wear your individual brand on your cap! You need to enumerate your career accomplishments, your core competencies, your success stories along with your education and accreditations. If carefully prepared and presented well, your UBE will focus on why you are valuable and more highly qualified than the competition. Are you are ready to build your unique brand equity (UBE) positioning to set you apart from the competition?

Chapter Three
Brand Identity

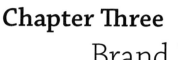

U.B.E.

Do I Require a Brand Identity?

Should I Consider Myself a Product?

The Answer is Affirmative!

Your "brand identity" delivers your value message. It is not just any brand—I want you to think of it as your Unique Brand Equity (UBE). It separates you from others in search and answers an employer's question, "Why should I spend time reviewing your candidacy over the hundreds of other qualified candidates whose resumes have come my way?"

Four Steps to Build your Unique Brand Equity (UBE)

Preparing your UBE takes effort and will seem difficult as you jump into this new positioning posture. However, once completed, it will become the basis of the marketing plan and selling effort for your candidacy. It will promote you more effectively to target companies and move you to preferred candidate status. Presented below are some ideas to get you started preparing your UBE.

> » **Core Competencies:** Focus on your specific and recognized leadership skills and your management

strengths. Think of those strengths as the reasons former colleagues in your career history counted on your leadership **and** counsel—in other words, how you became the go-to person. Realize that your competencies encompass both behavioral and professional elements. Be ready to demonstrate their interrelationship. Several possible examples may help to get you started in the process:

- Leadership in a strategic planning process
- Operations management and gaining stakeholder buy-in
- Improvement of processes and efficiencies
- Project and problem solution management effectiveness
- Negotiation and vendor management skills
- Start-up work and business development/revenue creation
- Communication success
- P&L management, taking care of the "bottom line"

» **Accomplishments:** These are the specific accomplishments and value you have contributed to your firm or team during your career. It is important to identify the metrics of what you have accomplished. Examples of typical accomplishments listed by our current clients:

- Team building reduced manufacturing cycle time by 30 percent
- $1.1 million purchase service agreement reached with logistic vendor
- "Green" branding added more than $500,000 in sales

- Strategic business direction helped cut expenses and increased gross margin 35 percent
- Process management system reduced staffing expenses by $500,000
- Statistical process control system saved more than $1 million
- Redesigned control panel which saved more than $6 million
- Negotiation leadership and technical research gained a $45 million contract extension
- Direct shipping eliminated delay, reduced inventory by $20 million
- Calculated risk in marketing expansion gained $1 million in new revenue
- Management system shift to business units reduced staff turnover by 40 percent
- Specific shipment guarantees gained preferred provider status at 14 mass merchandiser stores, big-box operations

» **Transferable Skills:** Most experienced candidates enter the process armed with an abundance of transferable skills. Senior management candidates usually are able to position their full range of capabilities to qualify for diverse work opportunities. Middle management candidates also possess transferable skills based upon early career and university activities that required a full range of leadership capabilities. Often those assets and skills can open doors and opportunities that may appear to be a stretch in terms of titles, job descriptions, or past organizations served. Using the full range of your qualifications can open non-linear paths to rewarding careers. Making use of transferable skills requires careful positioning to avoid the appearance of an unfocused career and a non-specific search plan.

» **Success Story Narratives:** Once you have responded to the direct questions in an interview, your success stories become the meat on the bone for your presentation. After defining your core competencies and accomplishments, you will separate yourself from the competition by stating, in an interesting and compelling way, your success stories. Where appropriate, include the transferable skills you used that could apply beyond the specific job opportunity. These success narratives will be most effective when they relate directly to the specific position being considered. I use the acronym SOARED as an outline for creating your UBE success stories, the vehicle I recommend for presenting your preferred candidate claim.

» **S**ituations
Obstacles
Actions
Results
Evaluative summary
Distinctive executive qualities

» **Situations:** Define in broad terms the background issues and complexities you had to deal with. State them succinctly in terms that show what you had to deal with in creating the success.

» **Obstacles:** The roadblocks that stood in your way and had to be overcome.

» **Actions:** The specific steps you took to deal with the situation and overcome the obstacles leading to the actual success.

» **Results:** State your results with an emphasis on the metrics you achieved. Prospective employers will want to understand how your results could apply to their organization. This element could be lowered revenue expenses, operational efficiencies, or improved team performance, among others.

» **Evaluative Summary:** Show how you were able to deliver the positive results you are proud to identify. This is the crucial component for being competitive in the search process. Be sure to use "I" versus "we" in your delivery, accepting major credit for your accomplishments where that is accurate. For those who are troubled by taking full credit, keep in mind that the "I" led the "we" to create the success.

» **Distinctive Executive Qualities:** These qualities—we call them your competencies—put an exclamation mark on your Unique Brand Equity! Make sure one or more of your competencies are incorporated into each of your success stories because they define you and your unique ability to lead and create solutions. This final element of the UBE formula can elevate you above the competition to preferred candidate status.

Your foundation piece, the UBE, will be your "selling proposition" used in all your networking efforts and marketing communications. You become the product and your UBE will be your value message for interested companies and networking contacts. Your goal should be to incorporate your UBE into all your communications.

Checklist for Using Your UBE

» Communicate your precise fit for the target company to secure the interview.

» Avoid concentrating on the number of jobs you have held or on your present or prior job title. Encourage the interviewer and other hiring decision makers to focus on your success stories rather than a chronological listing of your previous jobs. Concentrating the interviewer's attention on your UBE will be particularly important if you presently are out of work, have made many job changes, or are seeking to change your career area.

» Use your UBE to demonstrate your excellent potential for the position and the answer to the needs they have identified.

» Emphasize your ability to produce valuable results based upon your UBE.

To be the last job-hunting warrior standing, you must research each company in detail and define your skills as they apply to the position offered. In preparing your UBE, an essential step is modifying it to demonstrate how you meet or exceed the specs for each position and prospective employer. The organizational prerequisites may be explicit or implicit, but your candidacy hinges on an ability to interpret the company's talent search requirements to become the obvious winner, the chosen product in the competitive array of possible choices. More later about the techniques of delivering you UBE in a compelling way, to support your fit for the culture and chemistry of the target organization.

Chapter Four

Achievements

Competencies

W hat competencies displayed in golf can be compared to search preparation? I have seen, in over twenty years working with those in employment search, that many analogies can be drawn. Competencies, both behavioral and professional, are also known as skills, capabilities, or attributes. Whatever we choose to call them, many are winning keys to achieving goals in both golf and search. Let me list a few of the more than one hundred possible competencies published by Michigan State University Human Resources to illustrate the comparisons between golf and search. I find this list helpful to start discussions with my clients and I want you to see how these competencies may apply for your search process as well.

Golf Competencies	MSU Competencies For Search Clients
Must want to win	Ambition
Every golf shot is different	Dealing with ambiguity
Want to improve my game	Achievement desire
Courses demand good judgment	Analytical
New course, bad lie, new challenges	Adaptability

Fend off distractions to follow through	Composure under challenges
Enjoy camaraderie on the course	Communication/Likeability
Different holes require different strokes	Creativity/Inventiveness
Practice, practice, practice	Commitment/Work Ethic
Don't stop the swing too soon	Follow through
Make use of good coaching, feedback	Coaching/Collaborating
Commitment to shot and club selection	Decisiveness
Trust in the swing	Confidence
Follow ethical rules	Demonstrate integrity
Carry on when tired	Energized/Indefatigable
Weighs pluses and minuses in tactics	Broad sense of perspective
Know when coaching help is needed	Problem solving/New ideas
Handling the yips	Stress management
Dedicated focus on the game	Self-motivation
Dealing with slow play	Time management
Keep learning and trying, no give up	Tenacity
How a "righty" might need a "lefty" shot	Versatility
Able to recover from a bad hole	Resiliency

In 1994, as CEO/President of both First Career and Find Career, pioneering virtual career service organizations, I defined strategies and tactics to succeed in employment transition management. I counseled my clients that success in search required stating their unique qualifications. I wanted them to identify what we now refer to as competencies and how these competencies contributed to the success in their careers. In coaching sessions I asked job seekers to describe in writing the most memorable job-related success stories in which they were the key contributor. I wanted them to declare what they personally did in those events that they were proud of, the skills they applied and wanted to use in a new job position. We would then rank-order the skills they identified in their success stories until we had determined their most often used competencies. Those at the top of the list became the primary elements to emphasize in their documents and provided the support for their "superior candidate" claims.

Following that early rudimentary process, SCC-CT has taken the process to a more sophisticated and precise level today. Our staff chooses from an actual job description of interest to our client the core behavioral and professional competencies demanded by that opportunity. We match those job requirements to the individual's successful achievements and competencies. Those findings form the basis for in-office videotaped interviews during which our clients practice by presenting their success stories in simulated interviews with "prospective employers." Having researched the company and the job specs, our senior staffers and I play the roles of hiring authorities and decision makers. Listening and watching the recorded sessions of these simulations builds candidate proficiency and confidence. These recorded sessions are to be reviewed prior to real-world interviews they may face. By simulating interview sessions in our office, clients strengthen their self-confidence—another internal competency moving them toward their employment goal.

Your goal is to identify your competencies and to relate them in an interview situation. Start with an array of your success stories and see which of your competences stand out. Enumerate these competencies and use them to build your Unique Brand Equity (UBE). Make sure you can state with ease the competencies that meet or exceed the specific job requirements requested for your desired position. Build a repertoire of your success story narratives that emphasize what you did personally to make the success happen. Practice relating them to the potential employer clearly and effortlessly. By emphasizing how your achievements resulted from your competencies, you will be on your way to achieving your employment goal.

Chapter Five

The Scramble Yips

Self-Reliance

Don't Scramble Your Effort

In golf there is a fun team format called a scramble. Everyone in a foursome plays his or her individual tee shot. All players will play from the location where the best ball landed. Team members continue to play, always from the location of the last best shot, until one of the balls is finally holed. It is the ultimate team golf format with everyone rooting for their team members on each shot. The beauty is that you are able to rely on the other players because if you don't hit a terrific shot, chances are someone else probably will.

However, such a carefree attitude, and the luxury of relying on others, does not exist in the normal golf game or in career search. Counting on chance or someone else's actions can weaken your ability to rely on yourself when you are playing "real golf" or when planning your next career search. Remember, you are in charge of all your shots to reach the target—the job. In search, you are responsible for your own planning and execution. You need to focus on creating your candidacy's brand. That is the reason I discuss how to strengthen the presentation of your unique brand to create a winning candidacy that will help conquer your yips.

Chapter Six

Ordinary Cover Letter Yips

Memorable

Tee Up Your Search with the Tee Letter

" **L** et's tee it up!" is a suggestion that could not sound sweeter to an avid golfer. Teeing it up also offers promise of positive results for the serious career seeker. When job hunting, you can use encouragement at every step. In this chapter I suggest teeing up your candidacy with the "Tee Letter." It is a productive approach to getting your candidacy noticed, your career search process out of the rough and moving to an achievable chip shot to the green.

Once your search efforts have spotted a real opportunity, ambivalence and second-guessing may occur at the moment of document submission. Finally, after a long search, you have located the career opportunity of your dreams. You are ready to leap into serious competitive mode because the position you have found meets your career goals and you precisely match the position's specifications. But first, you have yet another critical step to take. You need to concentrate on an effective cover letter designed to accompany your resume, get your candidacy noticed, and carry your statement of interest it to the top of the applicant pile.

As everyone facing document preparation knows, the submission scenario can be daunting! There may be hundreds of applicants for one position; you want to be as competitive as possible getting your candidacy in front of the right people at the right level. After preparing your first draft, you start to revise and refine your cover letter and you begin questioning yourself:

Am I too intense? Sounding desperate?

Am I too generic/cut-and-paste? Appearing passive, maybe lazy?

Am I too serious? Contrived?

Am I too humorous or flip, lacking in judgment?

Am I too wordy? Sounding phony?

Here's my time-tested solution that will make your document a standout. Simple and straightforward, this approach with its successful track record is what I advocate to all engaged in search. I call it the Tee Letter, named after its T-like appearance when completed. At the top right, place your name, home address, contact numbers including LinkedIn (if it has been optimized) and date. Slightly below on the left, above the T, write the recipient's name, title, and full address. Use an appropriate greeting followed by a brief description of the position for which you wish to be considered. Now the T portion begins. In the left space list the primary specifications—their requirements that have been provided to you; in other words, the key elements of the job description for which you wish to be considered. On the right portion of the T, across from each primary specification, state your competencies and skills, both behavioral and professional, meeting those requirements. (Please check the sample Tee Letter at the end of this chapter.) Keep in mind that this format may be used at any time during discussions with a prospective employer. In fact we recommend that the Tee Letter should be at your side during interviews and referred to as needed during your presentation. It may be expanded and revised multiple times as you learn more about the position and the needs of the organization.

The Tee Letter establishes that you have read and understand the subject organization's needs as they have expressed them. It demonstrates your specific ability to match their needs with your skills and career competencies. It emphasizes that you can add value to them; and finally, it competitively separates your serious candidacy from the throngs of passive contenders. Please don't misinterpret my suggestion. This T-style letter is not the one and only method of presenting your candidacy. However, it is imperative that you design an effective covering letter in a format you feel comfortable with, using your own voice, words and writing style.

Beyond the published job description, where do you get detailed information about each company? You need to research using online sources, articles, opinion pieces, and annual reports to learn as much as you can about the company and what others are saying about it. This discipline helps you determine if your interest in the organization and the position is valid, meeting your goals and within your reach. Also, your search becomes more productive, interesting, and fact-based as you learn details and nuances of the organization. Armed with your research, your discussions with the prospective employer will prove that you are informed, have "eyes wide open," and are qualified to be hired.

Once you are ready to craft a Tee Letter for real target opportunities, here are suggestions to get you started:

1. Keep in mind that your goal with the cover letter is to assure that the reader actually spends more than 10 seconds on your full resume document. Realize that your correspondence may be one of many hundreds to be scanned or screened for the position. Using the company's key words that you have discovered in your

research helps significantly in getting past an initial rejection from scanners and into the call-back group.

2. Brevity is the watchword—two pages and no more than 500 words for this document.

3. The goal of your cover letter, of course, is to command attention for a closer inspection of your full candidacy using your Unique Brand Equity (UBE). You want to pique the reader's interest in learning more about you so that you will pass through initial screenings and into interview phases. The cover letter is not the document for relating your full career history. That will come. This step is to help you make the cut.

4. Your introductory comments must be simple and your basic rationale clear. Communicate the single-minded thought: "I am interested in presenting why I am fully qualified and a 'spot-on' fit for the position you are searching to fill."

5. Be certain your letter is tailored to the single situation you are exploring. Make it clear that you are focused on this one individual organization and opportunity. By using their stated requirements, you signal that you are not broadcasting your candidacy indiscriminately.

6. After comparing the position requirements to your abilities, be certain you see the fit is real before going forward. You must be convinced that your interest is a result of in-depth research and soul-searching. Use a no-nonsense approach; i.e., you understand what the job requires and therefore you are presenting your qualifying skills that meet their needs exactly.

7. As in all search correspondence, be certain your spelling is checked, names, and organizational titles are as correct as your context, language, and grammar. If in doubt about your use of language, use your computer or find a friendly English major to review it. Most screeners will not back a candidate who misspells, or misuses words and rules of punctuation. *Eats, Shoots & Leaves,*

The Zero Tolerance Approach to Punctuation by Lynne Truss is a delightfully humorous book that illustrates the need for careful use of commas and punctuation. Don't allow correctable language missteps to keep you out of the competition.

8. Keep in mind that your candidacy must be memorable and original. Communicate your precise fit in a succinct and positive light and the reader will be convinced that your other skills are as professional as your Tee Letter.

9. Finally, button up your Tee Letter with a sincere thank you for the thoughtful consideration you trust your candidacy document will receive. State that you will follow up with a phone call at a convenient time, offering a specific date for that contact. Then, keep your promise.

Consider using the Tee Letter. It is my recommended technique for gaining attention and increasing an employer's interest. Since many of my clients have used this type of document, I have proven that it can help candidacies move into the top tier interview rounds. So tee-up your candidacy and arrive on the green in regulation!

Sample Tee Letter

Your Name
Your Address
Your Phone Numbers
Your Email Address
LinkedIn Address
Date

Recipient's Name and Title
Recipient's Address
(If emailed or faxed, identify it as such and send a mailed copy as well)

Dear Mr./Ms. Employer:

In response to your search for a highly qualified Transportation Manager posted on Indeed.com, this letter presents my qualifications. I have compared the requirements for the position directly to my qualifications. I intend to illustrate both my fit for the position you have defined and my sincere interest in your organization.

Enclosed is my resume for your review. I believe that I meet and exceed your stated position requirements. I look forward to discussing my qualifications at your earliest convenience. I will call your office Wednesday morning, March 20, to request a mutually convenient time for our next step interview.

Very truly yours,
Your full name (signature)
Resume Attached/Enclosed

Transportation Manager, Worldwide Transports, Inc.

Your Requirements	*My Qualifications*
Scheduling disciplines/staff management	As Area Director, led six managers and a staff of 40 to develop over 22,000 weekly scheduled customers
Conversant with regulatory needs	Current with DOT, DEC, OSHA, and HUT requirements
Budgeting and financial planning	Constructed and administered annual budgets exceeding $55,000,000, including sales forecasts, expenses, accounts receivable, assigned P&L accountability
Five years-plus experience	Over eight years in the transportation industry, promoted within the past year to Central New York District
Bachelor's degree	B.S., Management and Marketing, SUNY, Potsdam

Chapter Seven

Competitive

Match Play Yips

Establishing Your UBE to Win

In many ways match play in golf is the ultimate test of competitive ability on the course. On each hole the player with fewer strokes wins. Each of the eighteen holes is a sudden death mini-game because once the hole is declared won or tied additional strokes are not counted and the players move to the next tee. The first player to win more holes than those remaining wins the match. The match play format showcases a golfer's skill on any given day competing against any given opponent. Also, sportsmanship is on display because a player may concede a putt if it appears the opponent is likely to make it. In conceding a putt, yips can crop up when the golfer asks himself, "Should I have done that?" or "I wish I hadn't." Match play creates and accentuates golfers' yips, and is particularly stressful for the player who falls behind in holes won. Competitive match play easily escalates into a debilitating head-trip and loss of confidence. Being behind in holes affects one's usual confidence and shot-making skills and can lead to giving up prematurely.

Let's compare "match play yips" to career search yips. Say you are competing for a position where you know the choice is down to several highly qualified candidates. You are questioning, "Am I the one?" Though you feel stressed, you need to avoid the yips and rise above the competing candidates. Here's how. Don't concede anything to the other candidates. Use your Unique Brand Equity (UBE) to give you an extra boost in confidence and eliminate the stress. Here are some preliminary suggestions to consider.

1. **Develop an arresting and compelling positioning that underscores your UBE.**

   A compelling personal marketing stance must demonstrate and communicate your preferred candidacy. The UBE is designed to stand out both in format and content by delivering the highlights of your competencies that have led to your career accomplishments. Tie both of them together to build the winning differences that will separate your candidacy from the competition.

2. **Underscore how your UBE is valuable, competitive, and fits each of the known needs of employer and position.** Your UBE should be comprehensive as it relates to the potential employer and builds your confidence as you state your value. It will present your qualifications for the position using your accomplishments, your competencies, and success stories. A UBE must be applicable to each targeted employer's stated needs or prerequisites. By presenting your unique brand candidacy to the organization, your effective UBE will go beyond addressing the job specifications and requirements and demonstrate your fit and potential value.

3. **Create a document that is relevant for each targeted position.** Take time to help the hiring side of the equation understand how your capabilities are relevant to their current needs. Generic, one-size-fits-all candidacies generally do not make the "must meet" list. Manage your message to demonstrate that you understand how your brand is the optimal fit for the employment being discussed.

4. **Present your UBE with strength, stating your career successes that address the prospective employer's needs.** This is no time to be reluctant or shy about presenting your career accomplishments. You must present your rationale to win as the preferred candidate. Remember, you are up against others who may be equally talented, highly educated, experienced, and proven performers.

5. **Demonstrate consistency and professional persistence in presenting your UBE.** You must not lapse into appearing or sounding indecisive in your presentation. Be consistent and focused in stating and emphasizing your fit for each of the employer's requirements. Then follow up the interviews or other communications with letters or emails demonstrating your sincere interest.

In today's crowded and highly competitive marketplace, prospective employers have many candidates to choose from. They need help in selecting talent from the staggering piles of resumes arriving daily. Resumes, those chronologically arrayed documents, may be useful as "calling cards," but they do not focus on your potential value to a company. A resume may pigeonhole you into a past position and limit new career opportunities. Don't be a resume blaster, casting your candidacy to the world and hoping it might stick someplace. The pitfalls of this practice will be discussed in later chapters. A well-prepared statement of your UBE is the platform you need to succeed. The interviewer will be helped in determining why you are the preferred candidate based on your professional and behavioral competencies combined with the cultural fit for the company. Your goal in "match play" searching situations is to win over your competition as early in the round as possible. Just as in match play, you need not win each hole—as long as you win more than the competition.

Chapter Eight
Blind Shot Yips

Creativity

The Hidden Job Market

Over the years and around the world, golf holes with "blind shot" tee boxes have not been popular. Golfers like to see where they are heading when hitting tee shots. Private golf club boards like to please their members and often make course changes to remove those pesky blind holes. For years my golf club in Connecticut had a first tee blind shot. The judgment our board made was that a blind shot on the first hole was unseemly for members and their guests, negatively impacting the start of their rounds. The solid granite ridge was bulldozed enabling golfers on the tee to view the flag on the green. Interestingly, when the project was completed I noticed no difference in handicaps ... if anything, they went up a notch!

Many in career search are under the impression that there exists some mysterious universe referred to as "the hidden job market." Are there subterranean groups of employment opportunities where a special password or a secret handshake is required? In my opinion, that is a fallacious idea. In our practice we work to identify potential opportunities that are not widely advertised. Some of these opportunities arise from companies experiencing dramatic growth, reorganization, or restructuring. I believe that the apparently hidden job market is caused by an organization's unannounced and often ill-defined need for talent. Companies may be working through the requirements they need for a new position before they are ready to post the job opening. I have seen potential new employment opportunities arise without a job description or before a hiring budget is approved. Many of our placed clients and their new employers tell us that the job description was created around the capabilities of the chosen candidate. That indicates the opportunity was "blind" until our candidate was introduced.

The answer to the "blind shot yips" is to be ready at all times to meet with companies who express an interest in you even if they say they are not actively hiring. A position may be created for you based on your UBE (Unique Brand Equity) and your well-presented candidacy. By establishing your competencies and how your abilities created valuable results, the organization may become enthused about taking immediate hiring action. If you are there at that moment, you may be the perfect "hidden" solution for the employer's needs.

Chapter Nine

Discipline

Lack of Preparation Yips

The Book in the Back Pocket

Watching golf, I am intrigued by the reading material that pro golfers rely on when preparing for their second or third shots to the green. Inevitably, I see them reach into their back pockets and lift out a skinny book that contains their scorecard, to be turned in after completing the eighteen holes, plus a non-digital compendium of other important information. The golfer must take care to enter his score since a careless mistake in stroke count places the entire round at risk and will cause a loss of tournament eligibility. But, what other information is in the book? Is it notes from *Harvey Penick's Little Red Book*? Inquiring minds want to know!

The most intriguing information is not the score. It is course detail that is studied intensely by both player and caddy before almost every shot is taken. The notes include the estimated distance to the green from a variety of spots on the course. In addition, the day's pin placements are noted and plans for shots from many spots on the course, both fairway and rough. Preferred landing areas on the green are precisely identified, taking into account slopes, ridges, valleys, and hazard risks. Even in this technological age, PGA tournaments do not allow lasers or measurement aids for golfers. Golf is wonderfully "retro," I think. Compiling all the necessary hole by hole information requires the caddy, and often the pro, to walk the course. They study it carefully in advance and write down the details with precision. Though perhaps apocryphal, my sources tell me that Tiger has been known to study details of the grass texture on the courses he plays. Apparently he believes that knowing the length and moisture content of the turf helps his club selection, direction, and swing effort. Watching the new top players as they chalk up multiple wins, I wonder if they too are using a similar level of preparation to gain shot accuracy and winning results.

Watching the pros reach for that back-pocket book, I see an analogy to what I counsel those in career search. Before every interview with a prospective employer, take time to "check your book" for the following key areas:

1. Walk the course imagining what you think the prospective employer will want and need to hear from you during the challenging interview shots.

2. Consider how you will react to the various people and their questions in the interview room.

3. Try to imagine the venue conditions and your ability to adjust. A one-on-one interview in a small space with HR will be considerably different from a panel interview with heads of functional departments.

4. Identify potential hazards in presenting your candidacy and how they may be avoided. Focus on your depth of experience and related competencies that will address a possible lack of formal education.

5. Take full advantage of your strongest attributes, your Unique Brand Equity (UBE), to make your competitive best shots.

6. Tee up the attributes you have that match the stated needs of the prospective employer.

7. Practice your swing, visualizing how you will use your achievement notes, compiled for that specific interview, and the optimal order to state them.

8. Carry the job description with you into the interview and place your key achievements alongside for comparison.

9. Emphasize those career success stories that will focus on your value for the specific company and their stated or implied needs.

10. Use advice and help in your preparation, making sure all parts of your candidacy are working in concert to prevent "lack of preparation yips."

Chapter Ten

Aim to Win

Winging It Yips

Practice to Groove Your Career Swing

On occasion, having been an unfocused golfer myself, I am aware that lack of practice leads to "winging it yips" on the golf course. To some casual observers, it seems like the game should be easy—stationary ball, motionless stance, no incoming curve pitches, nobody guarding you or trying to tackle you, and small probability of being hurt by your playing partners. Sounds easy. Still, golf is a most difficult game and not easily mastered. Golf shots involve demanding hand–eye coordination and require body parts to work in harmony in motions that often seem counterintuitive. To aid golfers yearning to improve their game, there are specialized high-tech golf clubs, each lofted and weighted with precision to fly a certain distance. More sophisticated and expensive clubs and equipment are purchased each season, with no appreciable improvement for the purchasers. No more than one percent of golfers are scratch or better, meaning, on average, they shoot par or better. So, expensive equipment alone doesn't make a good golfer. Golf, surviving for centuries pretty much as it was invented, is popular because every shot is different. Each requires a keen eye, creativity, athletic skill and, sometimes, more than a little good luck. Those who actually master the game have an abundance of natural skill but regardless, they continue to practice for hours each day. They set up a variety of shot challenges that could befall them on the course. It has been documented that Vijay Singh and other pros take well over 500 practice swings every day when not in tournament play. During tournaments, many players on the PGA tour go to the practice area immediately after playing a round to correct some swing defect that few of us would notice. They will not allow their game to fall victim to winging it yips.

Employment search is demanding too, requiring practice to become fully competent and ultimately successful. Few will achieve masters level in search tactics because, after all, acquisition of the job is the goal. No one wants to be known as an expert in looking for new employment! However, when laid off or changing careers, you need to be prepared to compete with tournament commitment. Search may be like the exam you had to take but rarely got around to preparing for. So, what to do? There is no script because situations are fluid and the interview questions come from all directions, requiring facility and confidence in responding. Like preparing for tricky golf shots, beating back the winging-it yips in search requires practice. As you would expect, I recommend that your practice is most helpful under the trained guidance and support of a professional career coach. It is also helpful to add friends with recent search success to your network.

Just as practicing tough golf shots can help win over the competition, having a prepared repertoire of your achievements and success stories, supported by your competencies, becomes the optimal way to search success. It is important to remember that your responses in interviews must deliver your measureable competitive capabilities on the way to becoming the preferred candidate.

Today's job interviews can be highly diverse in style, questioning, tactics, and topics. The interviewee must be prepared to face panels and individual grilling from various organizational levels and functional interests. A general, tell-me-about-yourself question asked by human resources or staff acquisition can be followed immediately by a specific technical probe requiring you to present your competencies. Questioners will go beyond *what* you have done, digging into *how* you did it. Interviewers will require that you present your value beyond the linear content of a chronological resume document. They may ask, "What competencies did you bring to the problem-solving effort that created your successful solution?" It helps to have taken several "practice swings" to prepare for those questions before they are asked.

So, the goal in preparing for the search interview is to practice responses to an array of tough questions until you are able, effortlessly, to relate your unique capabilities for the position. In my firm we ask our clients to participate in videotaped, simulated interviews in our office before "teeing off." We use actual job descriptions as the focus of our questioning. Though more friendly than the real thing, we are able to simulate the difficult questions we know our clients will experience in similar grilling in the real interviews ahead. The practice sessions, recorded and transferred to a flash drive for review with their executive coach prior to actual interviews, are extremely helpful to our clients in their preparation. Winging it yips can be conquered by answering some tough questions even before they are asked. Practice using these as starting points:

1. Describe yourself. Who are you professionally and personally?

2. What is the key element in this job description that created interest and moved you to apply for this position? Are you convinced that our organization may be a fit for you?

3. What are your unique qualities that make you a superb fit for this position?

4. Do you differentiate between work strategy and tactics? How?

5. What do you mean when you say "I am a good leader"?

6. Tell me why we should hire you.

7. Are there any reasons we should not hire you?

8. In defining the dimensions of an assignment, do you prefer to work alone before including your team? At what point do you bring your team into a project?

9. When setting goals for the team, how do you get them to "buy in"? Do they give you their honest comments?

10. How do you set timetables? Do you have an example of what you learned from a missed completion date?

11. What situations in a work assignment cause you worry?

12. How do you handle pressure? What was a worrisome problem that demanded your full attention?

13. What has caused you to get angry at work? How did you deal with it?

14. How do you define success?

15. Decision making:

   What steps do you take to arrive at a job-related decision?

   What is one of the most difficult work decisions you have made?

16. In your work history:

    What gets you motivated?

    What energizes you?

    What is an example of a project that you were passionate about?

17. What would they say about you

    if we asked your boss?

    if we asked your co-workers?

    if we asked your close friends?

18. Apart from talking about work, what about you would encourage me to want to spend time with you?

19. Among your many accomplishments, what do you consider one of your most significant successes? What did *you* do that made the success happen?

Keep in mind that practicing your responses to tough questions prior to your interviews will prepare you to emphasize your competencies, your unique qualifications, and your Unique Brand Equity (UBE). Winning the battle for preferred candidate status demands that you prepare and practice to avoid experiencing the winging it yips.

Chapter Eleven

Positive Preparation

Fear of Failure Yips

The Pre-Shot Routine Can Help

When approaching each shot on the course there are many opportunities to lose focus and fail. All kinds of issues can impact a shot—distractions from people around you, a weather shift, the lie, and conditions on the course. When talented pro golfers prepare for a shot, it is notable how they conquer their "fear of failure yips." They go through a regular routine of movements to calm their nerves and ease their stress. It is noticeable if they deviate from their regular routines. Unfortunately, some routines can aggravate the yips if they become too exaggerated or complicated. But, when well executed, they calm the golfers and help them avoid errant shots— for example, the dreaded straight shot when the intent is to draw left to get around a bunker or a fade right to clear a water hazard. The practice swing, the waggle of the club head and the slight press forward are common routine elements. These routines, by building shot confidence and calming the nerves, help golfers feel more comfortable addressing the ball. In my estimation each has a comparable application to job hunting where stress and pressure can crop up unexpectedly.

Getting into the interview conversation is not easy; I have seen experienced executives become flummoxed in initial interviews with prospective employers. You must avoid the obvious physical yips, like face touching, fidgeting, random hand movements and shifting posture as the interview commences. A yips example from our practice was a client whose widened eyes created distinct furrows on his forehead when he answered high-stress questions. We were able to point out to him that this wide-eyed stress manifestation overpowered his candidacy. Such yips signal discomfort and can become more memorable than your candidacy. To avoid awkward yips, find a comfortable routine for your search preparation, one you can use repeatedly to build your confidence. I recommend researching the company where you will be interviewing as step one of your "pre-shot" routine. Step two will be anticipating questions and practicing your interview responses. Beware of yips like nervously talking too much or too loudly. It is equally important to avoid awkward dead-air space. Keep in mind that a forward-press posture and good eye contact demonstrate that you are fully committed to moving the dialogue ahead. Now you are ready to present your candidacy calmly and confidently, making sure your interest in and rationale for the position are clearly communicated.

How do you avoid those initial physical stress manifestations I have mentioned, what I call fear of failure yips? Before each meeting have some neutral conversational gambits in mind, unrelated to the job itself, but designed to put you and the interviewer at ease. It is critical to begin the initial interview "dance" thoroughly prepared. I suggest a few below:

1. Topics of mutual interest from past conversations or emails

2. A positive comment regarding business or the economy relating to them and to you

3. Current events or sports; weather is okay as a starting point

4. Obviously, no politics or religion

5. Use visualization as step three of your preparation, imagining yourself in total control of your emotions during a perfect interview. Consider visualizing the following actions:

   - Finding a comfortable position that allows you to be relaxed and engaged
   - Making eye contact
   - Using the names of those you are addressing
   - Taking notes on the basic thought of each question asked
   - Remembering and responding to multiple questions
   - Asking for clarification when needed
   - Continuing to show active interest throughout the interview
   - Envisioning the conversation from beginning to end leading to a successful "swing" toward your employment goal

We work to protect our clients from entering into interviews without completing their pre-shot routine. How unfortunate it is to locate an opportunity, with your name written all over it, and fail in the first round of conversations! Just like golfers who require a familiar and calming routine to hit their ball well, job searchers will avoid fear of failure yips by instituting a preparation routine prior to their first interview.

Chapter Twelve

Goal Directed

Lack of Focus Yips

"Take Dead Aim," *Harvey Penick*

I am an enthusiastic subscriber to Mr. Penick's mantra for golfers to "take dead aim." In his *Little Red Book*, he offers advice that can apply to career search as well as to golf. My corollary is take dead aim when searching for employment. Golfers and job hunters who take dead aim are focused on winning. Mr. Penick opines, "Once you address the golf ball, hitting it with precision has got to be the most important thing to you at that moment. Shut out all thoughts other than visualizing the target and taking dead aim at it. Refuse to allow negative thoughts to enter your head. Swing away."

For a career searcher, my counsel is to adopt "take dead aim" as your personal mantra, a constant reminder to keep your focus on your target. Competing against the enormous numbers of others in search today, you need to spend your time effectively. The notion that a professionally written resume broadcast to the world of potential employers will deliver your job-hunting solution is wildly simplistic and outdated. You need a planned, focused approach because unfocused "resume-spraying" has been proven to fail in raising placement probabilities. It creates other negatives beyond signaling desperation. As an employer in search of talent, I occasionally received multiple resumes from the same candidate, arriving from different sources, with conflicting content and one-size-fits-all cover letters. Nothing turns off employers' interest faster than a widely circulated resume sent blindly and with little forethought. There are some 500 million resumes in circulation today. Thousands are sent daily to hiring authorities, recruiter organizations, and resume posting sites. Most resumes are subjected to initial electronic scanning and screening by administrators who use "checked boxes" to filter most resumes received, bringing forward only those candidates who fit mandatory prerequisites for each position.

Below is a list of problems that are caused by broadcasting resumes or submitting them to poorly researched targets where your candidacy does not meet their job description requirements.

» With the enormous number of resumes circulating daily, an unsolicited generic resume will be treated impersonally and risks never being read by a prospective employer.

» Indiscriminately sent resumes may be hijacked and forwarded to commercial operations who sell them to outside databases. This misstep may compromise confidentiality, especially important for those who are fully employed and searching quietly.

» Research to determine that the opening is current and valid. Time is wasted by unknowingly responding to previously filled, withdrawn, or outdated job postings— many are left online owing to employer and recruiter laziness or merely to add resumes to their databases. The massive number of outdated postings creates unproductive effort and frustration for searchers.

» Career firms have been known to solicit resumes and extract a fee pretending to have access to real job opportunities. Some state Attorneys General have established task teams to eliminate this fraudulent practice. Arizona is one state that works to regulate this unlawful activity.

The most aggressive resume posting websites, the blaster-sprayers, claim they will post your document for a fee to thousands of employers and recruiters as a valuable, results-delivering tactic. They promise your resume will reach worldwide job sites and assert that potential employers and recruiters will contact you. My recommendation is not to hold your breath for those calls to occur.

Getting executive-level candidacies to be noticed and evaluated by organizations with a good chance for an interview is an enormous challenge. I emphasize to my clients that over 80 percent of successful executive searches result from focused documents, persistent networking, and regular follow-ups. We understand that expanding our clients' networks of influence to build their campaign awareness is crucial. The optimal answer is to build and use your personal network, presenting your search statement so that personal introductions to potential employers are encouraged.

In order to obtain a personal interview, I recommend the following take-dead-aim actions:

» State your qualifications that present your specific fit for the position.
» Use your UBE (Unique Brand Equity) to support your success stories and transferable skills.
» Utilize technology to research current information about the target organization and the key contacts. Use their key

words in your communications so they know you speak their language.

» Determine the firm's preferred communication methods to follow up and maintain contact with all your networking contacts.

» Investigate what is known about their key executives and the firm's strategic direction.

» Explore how your competencies can contribute to the primary goals of the organization.

» Practice, practice, practice—as if you are preparing for the U.S. Open! Remain focused and take dead aim to assure your career shots do not land in the deep rough or hazards.

» Assume nothing until definite interest is expressed, then continue focusing on what you can offer—taking dead aim at every step of your search effort.

Chapter Thirteen

Adaptable

Misreading the Situation Yips

Understanding the Variables

You have your golf take-dead-aim attitude in shape and top of mind. You have made an excellent swing and your drive looks good. Now, there are at least three key variables remaining for you to consider:

1. The Lie—where my ball came to rest—can I advance it with precision in my next swing? Are there stymies that could impede my progress?

2. The Distance—what yardage is left to the target—which of my club options should I use to reach the final objective? Should I "lay up" to assure my next shot will be close and on target?

3. The Conditions—what are the challenges between here and the green—what is the impact of the changing weather? Mentally, is that missed putt going to affect my game going forward?

How do the above key issues pertain to search? When

you are off the "tee," and arriving at the next stage in the process of discovering and winning a new job opportunity, you will need to assess related situational issues.

The Search "Lie"

Golf requires a keen awareness of the lie of the ball in order to execute an effective second or third shot. Your best action will be to study a bad lie and calculate what to do to overcome it. What if your lie is in deep rough, behind a tree, or in a deep bunker? Taking a sideways shot to get back in the fairway may be smarter than taking dead aim from an impossible lie.

There are two comparable situations in search. First, if a request for your resume comes to you directly, a cover letter accompanying your resume needs to address this indication of interest. If networking sources or your personal initiative created the interest you will require a different cover letter. Be careful to check the "lie" of your of communications and choose the proper response. In Chapter 6, Ordinary Cover Letter Yips, I recommend a helpful tool, the Tee Letter. Using the "T" format, you will be able to tailor your response to most every type of job opportunity. Second, perhaps you have located a job description that seems to have your name on it. While preparing your Tee Letter, you discover that you must apply online. You have encountered an unfortunate impersonal "lie." Simply follow up the "to whom it may concern" impersonal application with one in writing sent personally to the key decision makers confirming that you also have applied electronically as requested. Express your interest in the position, emphasizing the fact that you have researched their organization. State that you can add value to the company and you want to make sure that your interest is not lost in the crush of the resumes that you believe will be flooding in.

The Search "Distance"

In golf, sometimes you realize the distance needed to reach either the target or to fly over a hazard will require more than one shot. Trying to execute one perfect, low probability shot is a risk you may choose to avoid. In addition, after four-plus hours on the course, the distance remaining to the end of the round can cause fatigue and loss of interest. Tension builds if all your interest is concentrated on "après golf!"

In search, a wise tactic to win the day is to be realistically honest about the distance remaining to a job offer. An overly aggressive pursuit may create the appearance of being too pushy, and may be too desperate in the minds of the hiring decision makers. Conversely, think of that outside rear view mirror on your car that suggests objects in the mirror are closer than they appear. Make a realistic assessment of the distance left to win the target job offer. The final distance is no time to lose perspective, focus, coordination, and staying power.

The Search "Conditions"

Conditions on a golf course are changeable. A storm during a tournament will cause the day's round to be delayed or cancelled. Slower golfers can hinder your sense of momentum. I once played a course where the rough had not been cut for a full week, because of rain. It was six to eight inches deep, so deep that balls hit there could not be seen until a golfer stood directly over them. Though experienced in playing from the rough, on one hole I had to use three strokes to beat my ball back onto the fairway.

I found six other balls in close proximity to mine left behind by other frustrated golfers ahead. Was I wasting strokes on a ball in an impossible lie? There may have been wiser options for the conditions I faced. Maybe I should I have called it unplayable and taken a penalty stroke!

During your search, conditions are likely to change, perhaps more than once. As prospective employers get close to making a hiring decision, the job specs can become more tightly interpreted or change completely. As the pool of finalists gets winnowed down, the original minimum requirement of a bachelor's degree may change to a demand for a master's degree. The required accreditation list can change. Compensation and relocation terms may have some "small print" surprises. Your patience will be challenged by changing job prerequisites. But, your justifiable frustration must be managed if you want to keep the opportunity open. Use your Unique Brand Identity (UBE) to emphasize your precise fit for the major aspects of the job description. Then assure the key decision makers that your interest in the opportunity is genuine and that you stand ready to assist them in redefining the offer terms and conditions.

By understanding the search variables described above, you will avoid the "misreading the situation yips."

Chapter Fourteen

Take Ownership

Begging For "Mulligans" Yips

Second Chance Do-Overs Are an Option in Practice Only

On the first tee in a friendly, non-tournament golf game, there is a longstanding accommodation for golfers to have a free "do over" second drive if they mess up on their first effort. This is called a "breakfast ball," "lunch ball," or "courtesy second chance"—also commonly called a mulligan. It is not allowed in the rules of golf but is regularly enjoyed by most amateur golfers, but only on the first tee and by mutual consent.

In a serious golf match, the rules of golf are observed and every stroke counts. Even an honest error on a player's scorecard or an unintentional rules violation, no matter how minor, is cause for disqualification—not just a penalty stroke or two. In friendly games with a small bet on the line, sixes scored as fives may be forgiven once in a while. But tournament play is a different matter because golf rules are definitive. Accuracy on stroke count and following the rules are not optional. You have to hit the ball from the spot where it came to rest or follow specific directions to take relief, usually with what may feel like harsh penalty consequences on your scorecard. No room for improving your lie or kicking the ball away from that pesky tree in your way! You must take a penalty stroke if the ball is unplayable or out of bounds. Because honesty and integrity are expected from and by all players, you are obligated to take your medicine and try to avoid repetition in the future.

I compare those stringent golf realities to a serious search effort. For instance, in search one can't pretend that a mistake did not happen. Mistakes, even unintentional ones, have consequences and there will be some degree of penalty. Intentional "mistakes" like fabricating education, employment details, or the reason for leaving your past employment will be found out and the prevarication will follow you throughout your current and perhaps future job searching.

There are no mulligans for negative initial impressions. Those mistakes will influence all that follows. I emphasize to my clients that, from the first interview to the last meeting, you must show a sincere level of interest in the firm and the position. You should try to be informed of the potential employer's business needs and the key people involved. Present a reasonably firm handshake, be presentable in your appearance, and demonstrate your enthusiasm for the opportunity. If you disregard these steps during the first meeting and act like you are waiting for a more interesting or important person to show up, you will create a poor impression. That may lead to never meeting the primary decision maker. Showing a lack of interest and readiness to fit the employer's culture and chemistry can kill an opportunity even before you are able to present your candidacy. It is important to establish your likeability with everyone you meet, not just the key players. All people in the interview process may be asked for an opinion regarding the first impression you made. Likeability is that intangible subjective asset you need to display to those on the other side of the hiring decision. They will be asking themselves,

"Can I see myself working with this candidate, attacking business issues together, and enjoying the process of collaborating?" That may be one of the most important elements of your candidacy.

Remember that at each step of your interview, those involved in the talent selection will be considering how they will be judged should they recommend you up the line to the ultimate decision-makers. Clearly, they will be asked, "What is your take on this candidate?" A lukewarm response from anyone you have met during your interviews, including administrative assistants, may knock you out of the running for the position you are seeking. So, prepare enthusiastically for each "shot" on your job hunt. Avoid aggressively pursuing situations when you realize a fit does not exist. Armed with your ability to deliver winning behavioral and professional skills and an informed interest in the position, you will not need a mulligan on the first tee!

Chapter Fifteen

Grasp Reality

Grip and Rip Yips

To Win Your New Position, Get a Grip!

Whenever my golf game seriously runs amock with little hope for rapid correction, I seek an objective point of view from a PGA teaching professional. After demonstrating my swing, I learn my grip is causing at least one of my several problems. My issue often involves a pull to the left, hurtfully referred to as a hook or, worse, a duck hook. The pro says, though my swing is strong, my grip has become too weak. As Harvey Penick in his *Little Red Book* reminds us, "If you have a bad grip with resulting off-target shots, the last thing you want is a good swing that will take those shots even further away from the goal." While other golf issues keep me and everyone else in my immediate circle of hackers out of PGA tournaments, correcting the grip is the step that helps my golf enjoyment and is a necessity for your career search success.

Job-hunting stress is magnified today thanks to the quantum number of top people in search, many with superb qualifications and preferred candidate status. In fact, the search game is more competitive now than it has ever been in the twenty plus years I have been assisting clients with career solutions. With the extraordinary magnitude of competition, searchers must be realistic about both their mental and physical grips. The physical grip or handshake is a very important aspect of your first meetings at the interview table. The second, a positive mental grip, is equally important as your campaign proceeds. Different as they are, if not fully understood each can be the kiss of death for aspiring job seekers.

The over-used truism, "you only have one chance to make a first impression," bears repetition here. Have you ever reached out your hand to meet someone for the first time only to be presented a "dead fish" or weak hand to shake? The limp handshake is unfortunate because it raises all sorts of questions. Does it imply that the individual is shy or lacking in confidence? Is this person bored, aloof, worried about germs or infections, or just not interested in meeting you? If the person immediately reaches for hand sanitizer, you have your answer! A weak handshake just raises too many questions. The other extreme is the powerhouse grip, the potential bone-crusher that feels like it might send you to your knees. No one appreciates a Charles Atlas handshake, unless you are searching for a position in heavy construction, one of my early summertime careers. Make no mistake, it is unwise to begin any first meeting with either a wimpy shake or proof you can crush a beer can with one hand. I also advise against the youthful, fun-loving fist bump greeting on your initial interview. It may be interpreted as arrested development or the signal that you are another germ-a-phobe. Non-traditional handshakes are fine when celebrating on the green after a long putt, but an unusual handshake can lead to a negative assessment of your executive capability. I suggest offering a neutral, comfortable, and confident grip when meeting new people in your search.

The second grip issue involves being sure that you are ready and qualified for the subject employment in most, if not all, the job specifications. Mental grip relates specifically to the career-seeker's individual psyche and ability to read the situation at hand. "Getting a grip" involves setting realistic objectives while keeping within yourself and avoiding trying for jobs and levels of responsibility that are out of your reasonable reach. Make certain that those interesting career stretches are supported by your body of experience, your progression through organizational ranks, your successes, your education, your technical accreditations, your competencies, and your third-party endorsements. Turn to my chapters on branding to prepare your Unique Brand Equity (UBE) document. With your UBE in hand, you will be prepared to express your fit and your transferable skills for the opportunity you are targeting. Keep in mind the following suggestions to make sure you have a grip on the job requirements and are sure it is a realistic career goal for you.

> » Make certain you understand the sometimes difficult to read demands of the search path you are on. Compare your abilities to what the organization says they want: the job description, competency prerequisites, degrees and accreditations plus work experience. Recognize the course conditions and the hazards you have to overcome in moving forward.
> » Work on each part of your "swing prep" and "pre-shot routine" and follow through with full confidence. Ask yourself: Will my documented success stories support my claim of being the best-qualified candidate?
> » Do I have the required professional, technical and behavioral competencies to perform? Am I able to express them clearly?
> » Can I, without hesitation, do the required work and perform to the company's standards?

» Will I be able to add significant value to this job and the organization?

» Am I a fit for the culture of this organization?

» Do I have the right chemistry to relate to and participate with their team?

When you have a grip on your search, you are ready to rip the competition.

Chapter Sixteen

Slippery Stance Yips

Stability

Establish Your Firm Stance Foundation in Golf and Career Search

For most golfers, a productive swing is neither comfortable nor easy to execute. It is quite different from other athletic endeavors and very difficult to master. Just ask me! The swing is measured in speeds that, for some talented players, are over 100 mph. In Bubba Watson's case, his swing speed is over 120 mph. That demands a balanced, firm platform to avoid falling forward or backward. The best way to avoid an embarrassingly uncoordinated flailing result is to focus on the stance. In golf this means getting the feet firmly and comfortably set and the entire body, arms and legs, to work in synchronicity to achieve a smooth swing and follow-through. The proper stance is critical when addressing the stationary small white ball on the tee or at an impossible lie on the course. Spikes on your golf shoes (soft or whatever course-approved type you prefer) are required to feel grounded and secure. They provide the foundation for your solid stance over the ball. The real key is to settle into your balanced platform, allowing all parts of your body to move in coordination, and swing effectively. The goal is to complete the swing with the belt buckle facing the target. Accomplishing this and maintaining balance and accuracy while avoiding hazards is definitely not an easy assignment to perfect!

Establishing a strong search stance, as in golf, is the critical factor for success in your candidacy. In my firm we discourage our clients from randomly jumping into interviews without getting their foundations set. To begin your employment search, the adage "get your feet on the ground" is certainly appropriate. You must form your search stance around more than the vague "I have a solid background. I am a qualified leader and a skilled motivator." Those are great claims, but they also echo many other candidates' claims. Consider availing yourself of coaching sessions in search. They are comparable to the spikes or nubbins on your golf shoes because they place you in a stable position, ready to swing with confidence as you search for your next employment.

Think about the foundation for your search stance in terms of four pillars. To resonate with a talent searcher or the hiring authority, you need to promote and sell your candidacy by stating your specific ability to add value to their job specifications. Your proposition should state more than chronological facts like past job titles, your verifiable education, and accreditations. The four pillars of your search stance should be:

1. Your known skills demonstrated throughout your career history.

2. Your documented achievements that were created by applying your competencies.

3. Your "problem/solution" success stories where you were the major contributor and leader in the achievement.

4. Your transferable management capabilities that can open new employment doors.

These four pillars are the basis of your Unique Brand Equity (UBE) and they support your claim to be the preferred candidate. Your UBE, once presented, will demonstrate the unique value of your candidacy. Your ability to present it with clarity for each prospective employer becomes your search stance. Now you are ready to "drive off the tee, split the fairway and advance the ball" on your job search course.

Chapter Seventeen
The All-Too-Speedy Yips

Rhythm vs. Tempo

As renowned teaching professional Jim Flick concludes in Golf Digest, "swing tempo and rhythm are not synonymous." Jim explains, "Tempo dictates the pace of your swing and rhythm relates to the order in which the many parts of your swing move to best effect." Jim then adds, "either a slow or a fast tempo swing may work well but only if based upon a precise and repeatable rhythm."

Some unfortunate events can occur once the golf club's business end starts moving in its approximately 18-foot arc, from the top of the swing down to the ball. When hands and the golfer's body get out in front of the club, the clubface will not be flush at impact. This "open" clubface may create a slice or, more kindly put, a push. Conversely, when a "quick" club head reaches the ball before the arms and hands, the dreaded over-the-top pull or hook will be the result. As Jim points out, by concentrating on your swing rhythm, your natural tempo will emerge. With practice, the shot result can be more consistently on target.

Jim Flick's golf coaching insights can help in career search as well. The thought of a lengthy, seemingly endless, employment search can create angst, family pressure, financial worry, and frustration. Understandably, getting a new job quickly is considered the goal by many. However, job hunters must focus on their rhythm in search and stop thinking that a speed-is-good tempo will succeed. My counsel for job hunters is to focus on getting all parts of a search program working in harmony, with a rhythm that doesn't get ahead of their ability to perform effectively.

A well-organized search process requires taking specific, well-thought-out steps with an organized flow and coordination to keep you balanced and grounded. Here are some tactics I find helpful to keep a search in synch:

» Carefully prepare your individual search strategy and tactical plans for each "employment shot." Your direction should point toward a reasonable target—one that is supportable by your education, core professional and behavioral competencies, and your past career successes. The tactical plan must start with a clear understanding of the employment goals you have set for yourself—for instance, job level responsibilities that fit your skills, a reasonable compensation package you can live with, an organizational culture and supportive work environment that will encourage your personal growth. Fundamentally, you must be convinced you will be able to contribute to the organization's success. It is also critically important to balance career and your family's needs. Starting off on a new career without family support is a sure invitation for rhythm problems. So, put speed aside until you are certain your personal stakeholders are on board with the situation.

» You need to be convincing in stating how your brand and competencies, your Unique Brand Equity (UBE), relate directly to the subject position and expectations of the hiring organization. Examples of these abilities include a record of motivating staff and establishing clear communication channels within past organizations. Having a record of accepting tough challenges and resolving issues to achieve valuable results is especially valuable if you can relate how you used your personal skills in achieving them.

» Emphasize how you used those unique skills to address specific, difficult, and financially critical situations.

» Focus on your career success stories that can build your presentation confidence and establish the credibility for your claims of past employment success. (One that is timely today is how you assisted organizations coping with restructuring and reorganizational issues.)

» Your preparation should include scheduled practice sessions and saying aloud the following: "My qualifications are based on my specific career successes. My achievements are directly related to your organization's needs and transferrable to challenging business conditions in the future. I am confident that I will excel in meeting your needs and goals."

Simply put, serious search efforts do not mesh well with rushing or a palpable sense of urgency. Develop your search rhythm to support your claims of being a preferred candidate in today's pressure-filled hiring market place.

Chapter Eighteen

I'm Stymied Yips

Overcoming Blockages on the Way to Your Employment Target

I n the early days of golf, there was no provision for relief when your ball came to rest blocked by another golfer's ball or by moveable man-made obstacles on the course. When that occurred, you were stymied! Back then, if faced with an obstacle on the way to the target, the only option was to jump over the blockage or hit to the side of it. Today's stymies are addressed in the rules of golf by allowing unattached objects to be moved and opponents' balls to be lifted, marked, and replaced to correct the blocked path to the hole.

Career stymies also crop up to plague job hunters. Searchers may be blocked when their career history fails to meet each of the primary specifications in the job description. For instance, if you don't have an advanced degree, a specifically required degree, or specialized accreditation, your resume may be rejected before it is fully read. A long tenure in your field of expertise may be interpreted that you are too senior and priced outside their salary range. Even a history of high level management positions in one organization may narrow the field of options because there is a general reluctance to bring in talent on a lateral or lower level. Being out of work for a number of months may place the value of your candidacy in question. Unfortunately, just being out of work may compromise employer interest, and a succession of short-term employments or consulting gigs may concern employers who are intent on hiring only candidates who have a full-time employment history. Being an entrepreneur and self-employed suggests to some that you might have difficulty adjusting to corporate life.

What are some answers for the stymies mentioned above?

1. After encountering a stymie in search, perhaps caused by a poor presentation of your capabilities or a missing competency, make every effort to get back in touch with the decision makers and present your candidacy in terms of your Unique Brand Equity (UBE). This can answer many of their concerns.

2. Once you have gained hiring interest, the single strongest move is to focus on your list of accomplishments rather than the chronological time line in your resume. Delivering your success stories in your UBE will show how your professional competencies fit the individual employer's requirements and will be of value to their firm. This approach can "open up the course" to your employment target by overpowering any stymies.

3. Lastly, I counsel you to keep up the momentum. Demonstrate through your success stories how the behavioral and professional competencies you possess and the successes they created far outweigh any stymies that block your candidacy's success. If presented as the reason for your successes, your stories of achievement can eliminate the stymies.

According to Department of Labor statistics there are over 20,000,000 unemployed or under-employed persons in the U.S. Though potentially employable, some aspiring career hunters, when told repeatedly that they fail to meet job specs, merely give up searching and choose to quit and wait for better times. There are others, about 15 percent of the potential U.S. workforce, who are frustrated but have accepted jobs that are stop-gap, low pay or temporary in nature. Meet those stymies head on. Focus on well-prepared and rehearsed rationales from your UBE that can overcome the blockages to your employment goals.

Chapter Nineteen
Wits' End Yips

Positivity

"To Conquer Golf Yips, Go to Dinner with a Good Golfer" *Harvey Penick*

"When in Search, Hang with Positive People" *Chuck McConnell*

A voiding the dreaded three-putt is an ongoing challenge once your ball is finally on the green. A string of missed putts can get you thinking you have lost your touch. The harder you try to conquer your yips, the more pronounced your stress gets. You start talking to yourself. Sometimes others start offering conflicting stroke suggestions and the negative multiplier effect kicks in. The "wits' end yips" may be conquered by golfing with players who play somewhat better than you. Years ago a club teaching pro told me that I had to play with better golfers if I truly wanted to improve my game. If they are calm, supportive, and confident, successful players will help improve your game by settling your stress. This learn-by-example formula is excellent advice as long as the better players are patient and friendly.

In a similar way, search efforts prosper when the atmosphere is as stress-free and positive as possible. When the wits' end yips afflict you, the best answer is to network and spend time with positive people and those who have succeeded in their career search. Addressing each search challenge with a positive attitude combined with upbeat feedback from those around you is a winning strategy. My counsel is, don't rely exclusively on networking and associating with others who are unemployed or currently in search. It may be too easy to lapse into a mutual "ain't it awful" session. You need to balance attending career search meetings with an equal number of conversations with those who have already succeeded in their searches. Of course, every opportunity you pursue will not result in winning a terrific new job offer. Your efforts should not be win–lose situations because each is a learning opportunity. Positive group discussions encourage positive attitudes. So you must strive to enter each new exploration with fresh insight and enthusiasm.

Knowing that you have had many interviews and failed to make the final cut in any is difficult. How and with whom do you share your concerns when you are feeling challenged in your career search? Avoid people with judgmental comments like "That was dumb" or "You said *what?*" Beware the damaging and somewhat suspect comment, "You are too good for them; they were threatened by you." Judgments like these and the quick solutions offered sound more like reprimands or lame excuses and will offer you no help. You need a supportive ear from someone you can confide in and who will really listen to your concerns.

Born in the 1960s, the human potential movement proposed multiple strategies, short of psychological analysis, to face inner struggles and negative or defeatist attitudes. One of these strategies, and my recommended solution for the wits' end yips, is seeking out friends who are active listeners. Don't the following comments from dedicated active listeners sound more helpful? "I hear you." "I understand." "Say more about your interview concerns." Look for active listeners in search networking partners, close friends, and career coaches. An effective active listener will *really hear* you. They do not stop with the facts of what you did and said. They will ask good questions in order to learn about the situation and how you are dealing with it. They will not reprimand or offer unsolicited advice. With a skilled active listener you will have an opportunity to share your thoughts, review your actions, and focus on some of the fundamental issues that may be getting in your way. An active listener may say something like, "Here is what I think the interviewer's comments were getting at. Let's see how those comments might be helpful in moving ahead." One of our SCC-CT clients, having experienced a year of fifteen interview rejections, came to us demoralized. Despite an outstanding executive history, he was showing defeatist tendencies. He was able to share details of his past interviews with our coaching team and receive their feedback. With supportive active listening, his confidence returned, leading to a strengthened campaign and a positive outcome.

A skillful coach listens actively and interprets the reasons for search stress before offering any advice. Using a qualified coach enables you to recover from search disappointments and helps you focus with purpose on your revised search efforts. Acting as a sounding board, your coach will play back, in a different voice, your concerns. Once you are helped to recover and regain your positive attitude, you are ready to process examples of successful tactics that have proven helpful for others. You become reenergized for the continued job-hunting process.

Spend time with positive people and seek out active listeners for your next search opportunity. You will progress to the next tee with strengthened confidence and resolve, having corrected the wits' end yips.

Chapter Twenty

Perceptive

Speed Estimating Yips

There Is No Search Stimpmeter

O nce a golfer has finally arrived on the green, the challenges continue through to the hole. Most of us mere golfing mortals can take well over half of our total strokes on or close to the green. Because golf greens vary from one course to another, an ability to adjust is required as one tries to hole out. For those non-golfers at a loss, let me define speed estimating before I explain how it applies to the search process.

The average ball roll speed varies tremendously from course to course due to greenskeepers who determine the type of grass planted, the length of the cut, and whether or not the green has been rolled. Even the age of the green and the time of day will affect the roll of the ball. As opposed to PGA tournament courses, most present-day golf courses do not measure or post the speed of their greens but it is one of many important variables in the game. About 80 years ago at a location close to the birthplace of the game in Scotland, an innovative golfer, Edward Stimpson, chose to measure differences in green speed on the various courses he played. Stimpson created the Stimpmeter to help golfers adjust their putting strokes based on the green speed. He made a simple wooden ramp with a 20-degree incline to be placed on a flat green area. A golf ball was released on the ramp to determine the distance it would roll. The average distance on six consecutive tries, north and south, was measured and declared the "Stimp" speed of the green. That somewhat rudimentary measurement tool, though refined, is still used today in professional tournaments to give pro golfers a sense of how the ball will react to a putt—somewhat imprecisely, but a help nonetheless. Very slow greens have an average Stimp rating of 4 feet; fast greens average up to 10 feet. But the most difficult major tournament courses such as Augusta and Oaklawn have super-fast greens that may, on any given day, exceed 12 feet. Even if average golfers were able to use a Stimpmeter to determine ball speed, they would still find putting a challenge. Who said golf was easy?

I often hear requests from job hunters who would like to know the precise speed of their search. Stating a definite time frame in weeks or months is impossible because there are too many variables in the process. The need for speed may vary because of economic uncertainties and changing hiring decisions. Though somewhat predictable in times of near-full employment, the speed and time required to secure new employment is impossible to estimate with accuracy today. There are more variables in search than on the golf green and any attempt to develop an accurate "search-meter" is impossible. In predicting search speed for our clients, we offer a range of possibilities. We have documented wide variances in the speed of search during our years of serving those in transition. The mean average search time for the total universe of our clients, ranges between five to six months. Because they have insufficient time to devote to the process, many fully employed clients take longer for their job search. They need to maintain confidentiality to avoid placing their current employment at risk. Conversely, the unemployed have more time and usually complete their search preparation more rapidly. But they may experience slow decision-making by prospective employers or they suffer from the current bias against out-of-work candidates. They may face prospective employers who offer lower-than-market compensation packages, taking advantage of an unemployed candidate's urgent need to get back to work.

We believe that speed in search should not be your primary goal. By arbitrarily setting that as a target, you risk accepting a suboptimal employment offer out of frustration. The old search maxim of "a month of search for every ten thousand in expected base salary" is not useful today. That is why it is more important than ever to bring a professional resource into your job search campaign, making the speed of your search a result rather than the objective. Using skillful professional counsel provides an objective point of view, opens up new options, and widens the scope of your search.

Accurate prediction of search speed is truly an impossibility. Just like a too-slow putt stopping just short of the cup or a fast putt zooming past the cup, managing search speed can be equally frustrating. I counsel that no one should set a definite time expectation when looking for new employment. Search success will occur if your expectations are kept realistic. By following the procedures outlined in this book, you will avoid the perils of "speed estimating yips" and the timetable to your target employment will take care of itself.

Chapter Twenty-One
Misfit Yips

Discerning

Assessing the New Situation

O ccasionally when pairings are made on the golf course, you may find yourself in a foursome with total strangers. That can be a wonderful experience or not. Some newly met golf partners are immediately likeable, friendly, polite, and accommodating. Meeting new people on the course is a good time to test your social skills and assess your ability to deal with diverse types of people in stressful situations. Golf can uncover some difficult personalities behind the golf club including lack of affability. Why? Once again stress rears its ugly head and dealing with that stress can be challenging. Surprisingly, lessons learned in being thrown together with another golfer or two can become helpful experiences that lead to winning in career search.

It may be that my Myers Briggs personality type, ENTJ (Extraversion/Intuition/Thinking/Judging), contributes to why I usually welcome meeting and being paired with new golfers. I appreciate considerate playing partners with positive attitudes and a sense of collegiality. I readily admit, however, that other golfers' idiosyncrasies can be challenging. My silent complaints may be: "They play too slowly." "They take too many practice swings."

"What, start the morning round with a cigar and a beer?" For me, one of the most objectionable personalities is the rules-of-golf fanatic whose stream of assumed authority, often incorrect, can be tiresome. Then there is the angry, club-throwing golfer whose frustrations, though understandable, are often blamed on their playing partners. I avoid the self-absorbed player, the rude-nik, who tells a joke while another player is preparing to swing. How an individual relates to others on the course, including in the pro shop, with the starter, the caddy, and drink wagon people can be personality clues. I once played with an oaf who thought it funny to proposition the young lady at the drinks cart. She did not appreciate his hung-over humor and the encounter was embarrassing for the rest of us. The offender was permanently relieved of his club membership soon afterward.

Being introduced to new golf partners is not unlike first meetings with potential employers or their staff. Golf is a helpful laboratory for determining the type of personalities with whom you want to work and collaborate. My advice is to recall your golf course encounters as you meet and deal with various potential employer personalities. In the interview, they will be assessing you while you are observing them. The astute searcher can determine a great deal about fit based upon the entire interview process, not just the Q and A's. Occasionally, you will be introduced to somewhat formidable characters—call them talent acquisition spokesmen—who may be outstanding in their work skills but surprisingly offensive or disconnected in their interviewing approach. That is when your assessment "nose" must get involved. You need to assess how the new job, should it be offered and you accept it, will evolve during future stressful times. Your decision depends on your ability to read the players who represent the organization. This requires a keen perceptive sense to predict how you can be effective working with the full array of personalities at the new organization. Be aware and notice how prospective employers relate not only to you but to their co-workers as well. Have you been welcomed and treated professionally as a potential employee? Are they presumptuous, rude, uninvolved, or condescending? Are they interested in you, the person, in addition to your professional skills? Can you see the chemistry being as positive for you as it is for them as prospective employers? Job offers will be determined by the hiring authority, the individual in charge of the search process, who may become your future colleague. Your ability to contribute will depend on how effectively you will function in the team environment created by that decision maker. Be cautious if you cannot see and sense the basis for a mutually good fit.

Search success is difficult to achieve if you don't consciously make an effort to assess the personalities you encounter and decide if the position is right for you and your management style. The prospective employers will be asking themselves, "Can this candidate do the work? Will this candidate thrive in the chemistry of our company?" You need to ask yourself, "Will this company's management create the right chemistry enabling me to contribute and grow? Will I be able to use my competencies to best effect? Will I enjoy working with these potential colleagues?" Answers to these questions will test the position's suitability for you. You can avoid the "misfit yips" by carefully analyzing your new job opportunity and the people with whom you will be associated.

Chapter Twenty-Two
Slow-Play Yips

Advance

Looking and Moving Forward with Purpose

S low play on the golf course and being hit into by the group behind leaves golfers mumbling and looking for the ranger to register their concerns. I have witnessed golfers who have been hit by balls—one who experienced a concussion. This is not desirable during what has been called a wonderful walk in the park. Slow play, either in the group ahead of you or in your own foursome, can cause a break in one's concentration. A round of golf is played comfortably in 4 to 4½ hours. So a 5½-hour round will turn most golfers' smiles upside down. Most golfers become irritable after an errant ball lands near their foursome. Sometimes, the recommended and helpful "FORE" will not be heard. But usually the guilty party will offer apologies and a "Sorry, that was a career-long shot!" That is better than nothing but it is a feeble mea culpa at best. However, those on the incoming side know, deep in their "range finder" hearts, that the close call may have been caused by their own slow play. These "slow-play yips" are analogous to issues in search where one must focus on moving forward with determination.

I played a final tournament round with an otherwise nice

fellow who insisted on checking random distances with his range finder on every shot—to the hazard, to the rock, to the willow tree at the dog-leg. Clearly, his confidence was built on precise distance awareness. He did not seem to care that his measurement equipment is designed, primarily, for estimating distance to the pin. For the PGA pros on tour and on some club courses, the range finder is verboten. Because of the lengthy time my opponent spent measuring unimportant distances on the course, that round lasted 5½ hours and I lost on the sixteenth hole. I was worn to a frazzle and hoping the pro following us would penalize my opponent for exceeding the shot-prep timing policy. Somewhat reluctantly, I accept most of the blame because, as I describe in the chapter "Between the Ears Yips" I was unfocused and let the slow play get to me.

So how does slow play relate to job search? Slow search progress can result from trying too hard, being numbed by multiple rejections, losing determination, trying too many new tactics, or merely a lapse in confidence. Those who continue in search with no results may have fallen victim to the slow-play yips. Contrary to the Department of Labor statistic of approximately 6 percent unemployment, I believe 15 percent of potential U.S. workers are "un" or under-employed today. This differential is due to actual U.S. workforce participation which hovers around 63 percent and is the lowest since 1978. Apparently, many have lost motivation and dropped out of job searching. Some say they are waiting for better days. If today's sluggish economic growth returns to to an annual 3 to 4 percent GDP growth rate that will encourage more certainty and robust employment growth.

Like most mental and physical endeavors, search thrives on forward momentum. A sense of regular pace in job hunting contributes to confidence. When search stagnation occurs, you risk loss of focus, interest, and heart. It is very easy to wheel-spin, reverting to using the same failed tactics for every new opportunity. Unfortunately, protracted search can become debilitating. When the same poor result occurs from taking the same action over and over, I am reminded that Einstein defined that as idiocy. However tempting, do not be a victim of the too-speedy yips, described in another chapter, where you might be tempted to substitute tempo for rhythm and momentum.

"Play it forward" is another golf term that applies to keeping momentum. By using the forward tees in golf, the game can be accelerated, made more forgiving and pleasant. Course designers and many PGA professionals believe that most courses should allow golfers to improve their games by reaching the green, or close to it, in no more than three strokes. Likewise in search, by using a forward-looking professional process, you can create and maintain momentum. If you are stalled, look for a credentialed professional coach who knows how to stimulate your progress by helping discover effective tactics and more productive answers. Don't let momentum sag and you will reach that nineteenth-hole reward, the new employment you are targeting.

Chapter Twenty-Three

Low-Tech Yips

Technology is Vital to Search Success

T he United States Golf Association (USGA) is the body that interprets and approves golf equipment specifications. The association has been challenged the past twenty years by club and ball innovations that would have had heads spinning in old Scotland! There have been huge technical advances and changes in the equipment used, virtually each year. Modifications to drivers, fairway metals, rescue clubs, and wedges with computer-designed grooves to maximize ball spin have been introduced by leading golf manufacturers. Cynics suggest that some innovations are related to marketing rather than golfer performance. But occasionally, those creating and innovating to push the envelope actually give golfers better shot accuracy and scoring results. Mechanically adjustable drivers that minimize errant shots have made the game more manageable. Longer and more flexible shafts have helped seniors get more distance off the tee. However, during the past decade the USGA has stepped in to regulate some extremes, including the use of long shaft putters and square grooves on wedges. Also reined in have been innovations to drivers with extreme "trampoline effects" that are designed to enhance distance. These are extraordinary advances in an ancient sport that started with simple leather balls filled with feathers and clubbed by clunky wooden mallets! "State-of-the-art" shafts of bamboo were once seen as advanced technology. The driving force behind these techno-advancements, besides the bottom line of the manufacturers, has been the decision to help players become more competitive, hit more consistently, score better, have more fun, and overcome their yips.

Search for employment also has advanced through technology. It was once a process that relied mostly on print advertising to build awareness for job openings. In the world of job search using technology is necessary now for gaining competitive advantage in your job hunt. The digital world now requires job hunters, for better or worse, to become major users of instant electronic communication. What this technological revolution has encouraged is an enormous growth in the number of participants in search. Ten years ago the majority of searchers were unemployed or underemployed. Today, owing to the decline in loyalty for both employee and employer, we see a dramatic increase in the number of fully employed people searching for new situations. In my practice, nearly half of my clients are currently employed. The quantum number of resumes being floated combined with the mechanical and impersonal screening of these resumes has been an unfortunate result of the current technology. Because of that exponential growth, even well-crafted search documents may never be read or scanned beyond the top third of the first page.

Conventional wisdom for a large number of people today is to keep all their job search options open, even if they are fully employed. That has caused uncommon competition for the all-too-few prime jobs available. The unemployed are pitted against those looking to change from current jobs. Adding to the pressure, a submitted resume often seems to disappear into a black hole with no response from the employer. Employers' failure to respond to resumes has created negativity and frustration, causing many to drop out of search. The level of national workforce participation has dropped to less than 65 percent, the lowest level since the 1970s. That is why, despite a lowering of national unemployment statistics, we have over 35 percent of prospective employees giving up the pursuit of new employment. Despite all the issues in our present day search climate, it is mandatory to make effective use of the internet and technology for ultimate search success. Nearly half of the searching population has little interest in knowing how to use electronic media and unfortunately, absent that effort on your part, you may be lumped into the Luddite category.

Networking is the most valuable tactic searchers need to employ in a job search because it is directly or indirectly responsible for over 80 percent of all hiring success. We encourage our clients to use the internet to research details for any target organization before taking an interview. We strongly advocate using the networking and research capabilities of LinkedIn, a social media resource that goes far beyond merely linking you to other people. Both employers and recruiters searching for talent regularly access this useful medium. We help our clients optimize their profiles on LinkedIn and take advantage of its full value. We advise our clients to respond to connection requests because those contacts are often helpful in building a communication bridge to potential employment opportunities.

Our firm has an internal network of influence with organizations and individuals that we have served and we tap them for our clients when appropriate. Our goal is to help clients avoid false hopes and "wheel spinning" by showing them how to selectively use the internet and social media to accelerate the search process. So, by all means, improve your chances for new employment by using the internet and social media and make sure you don't suffer from "low-tech yips."

Chapter Twenty-Four
Un-likeability Yips

Civility Leads to Likeability, a Necessity in Search

After eighteen holes of enjoying golf and its challenges, golfers want to leave the course with good humor and friendships intact. In golf's long history, a tradition of civility, integrity, and comradeship has been established. Having watched each other deal with hazards, frustration, lost balls, and impossible lies, we are ready to leave our frustrations on the course and enjoy some camaraderie at the nineteenth hole. It is the quintessential "Rockwellian" golf picture, at least for me and my golfing buddies. If edginess or disagreements, some requiring an apology, crop up on the course, we seem able to recover quickly over a beer and avoid the "un-likeability yips." Often we say with a smile, "It was a good round, nobody got hurt, and we did the best we could on the course with what we had!"

Surely you have noticed on television or in person that pro golfers have the ability, no matter the adversities they faced on the course, to end the round graciously with both their playing partners and caddies. With a smile, a gracious pat on the back, and friendly handshake, they leave the eighteenth green with civility. We watch transfixed when pro golfers make major errors in the last few holes of a very close match—errors leading to a loss and financial hit that might exceed the GNP of some small countries! One marvels at their composure with hats off delivering gracious end-of-the-match congratulations to their opponents. Observing the pros offering their hand to opponents, win or lose, makes me feel proud to be a member of the golf community. I am reminded of the military salute, the visible sign of friendship and respect—an old-fashioned, "I enjoyed sharing this round of golf with you."

Now I ask you to consider how likeability, as seen in golf, can help you in search. You need to be self-aware and introspective to make sure your personal likeability is kept intact. I am proposing in this book that job hunting encourages stress and stress can escalate rapidly into yips. Obviously, it is mandatory to not lose your cool and say things under pressure that you will regret. Despite non-committal interviews and candidacy rejection setbacks, civility and likeability are necessary assets as you regroup and move forward in your employment campaign. Regardless of how you think the last interview went, even if you think you blew it, the final handshake and thank you, both personal and in writing, are essential. Maintain your likeability quotient and you may keep the company's door ajar for future communication. A recent client's experience is interesting. He received a negative assessment and rejection one day followed the next day by a request to catch a plane to meet that organization's board. Since he never burned his bridges with negativity, his winning attitude kept him in the running for the second round and a new chance for search success.

There are several ways to build likeability:

1. Use the names of those interviewing you.

2. Balance your self-assertiveness by asking questions as well as answering them.

3. Show your humanity and the lighter side of your personality.

4. Be aware of their timing and help them keep to their schedule.

5. Smile appropriately and work to be on their wavelength.

If you are rejected or you feel that an interview went poorly, keep all avenues open through your timely follow-ups and thank you letters. Things may not be as bad as they appear. Recognize that the FEAR factor (False Evidence Appearing Real) may be at play. Don't underestimate the opportunity for reconsideration. Another meeting or an even more advantageous situation may follow based on your positive attitude that created rapport. Being resilient and not losing your confidence after a difficult interview is important for your job-hunting process, as well as your mental health. However the job opportunity plays out, learn from each experience and continue to monitor your interpersonal skills to avoid the deadly un-likeability yips.

Chapter Twenty-Five

Energized

I Can Coast Yips

There is No "Quit" in Golf or in Search

Committing to hitting a golf shot is much like committing to the job-hunting process. Both endeavors have similar and comparable potentials for disaster. Let's see, lost ball/lost resume; penalty for hitting into a hazard/penalty for offering inappropriate responses to interview questions; missing the green due to faulty pre-game preparation/faulty positioning of your candidacy due to a nonchalant search attitude. These are the "I can coast yips" occurring when your conclusion is, "No problem, I'm a contender. With my degrees, past job titles and references, I will win the day." As golf legend Greg Norman has said, "There is no 'quit' in golf." To that I add "or in searching for your next career." Greg offers other words of wisdom that I believe can apply to your search. I paraphrase them here: you must be fully committed and you must learn to deal with success and failure. The game of golf is challenging and you have to work and practice with commitment, perseverance, and determination.

Greg says he was never fearful on the course because he was determined to be prepared and committed, an attitude that led to his successful record in competition. One way that Greg followed through on his "no quit, no fear" mantra involved his emphasis on precision game research. His shot planning and club selection were superbly accurate primarily because his caddy gave him estimates for his shots in half-yard increments—not 120 but 119.5 yards. Thanks to this planning and preparation, he made it to the green in an excellent position to have a "good chance" versus a "no chance" putt. Greg kept his positive mental attitude. Even if fading on a Sunday in the final phase of a golf tournament, Greg was determined, persistent, and always ready for the next challenge.

Applying Greg's example to your search, I suggest that succeeding in search demands confidence born out of effective preparation. Bring a positive mind-set to your best efforts. Win or lose, your mantra should be "In all my efforts, I will do the best I can every step along the search path." Don't coast in your efforts because overconfidence is your enemy in job search. I recall that in my advertising career I once worked for a CEO who gave everyone pins to wear that were in the shape of a stop sign. On the octagon were printed the words, "Don't Stop." That odd, yet attention-grabbing message should apply when you are searching for new employment. Don't stop! Keep working to avoid errors of omission, commission, and overconfidence. Job hunting success rarely results from luck. Coasting at any stage can turn into lost momentum and a downward spiral that destroys confidence.

Chapter Twenty-Six

False Front Yips

Handling Surprises in Search

T he flag marking the cup on the green is the penultimate target in golf, usually eyeballed with some degree of certainty from 100 yards out. Greens, with hazards lurking like minefields, present more than enough difficulty for any golfer. Turtleback putting surfaces, slopes, swales, unrepaired ball marks, water hazards, and bunkers guarding the edges or even in the middle of a putting surface will challenge all golfers. But occasionally, there are other potential problems to worry about, ones hidden in plain sight. I refer to the dreaded "false front" golf green, a truly diabolical obstacle that causes yips both before and after a shot. The false front is an area that, when viewed from a distance, appears to be the flat apron in front of the green. The golfer tries to land his ball there thinking it will run toward the hole for an easy putt to the cup. In reality it isn't flat; it is an area inclined toward the golfer. Alas, hitting that slope on the false front may redirect the ball back to the golfer's feet. The misread of a false front is nearly certain to turn a birdie opportunity into a bogie or worse. Dealing with false fronts has caused many golfers to suffer the "false front yips." Television viewers watch sympathetically as pro golfers tackle treacherous false fronts like holes 4 and 16 at Augusta National, home of the Masters Tournament.

Job search presents a similar dilemma. Imagine the following scenario. The initial meetings and positive interview feedback looked like a straight roll to success. You read signals suggesting you made the first cut. Other explicit comments from the hiring side seemed to indicate the job offer could be yours. Then, out of the blue, you are informed that you are not among the finalists. Huh? Why? What did I miss? Did the decision maker have a predetermined candidate? Was it something I said? Was my interview just a legal diversion? Am I overqualified or did I seem too expensive? Is it my age? Did I not "click" with the key decision maker? You may never know the answers, but you know the "search-ball" is back at your feet.

A positive mind-set must return as you get set for the next "swing." But first you need to review the events to be certain you are able to avoid a recurrence. A post-mortem, objective review of the event is useful. Do a reality check to determine if the fit and rationale for your candidacy for that situation was correct. Assure that your interpretation of leadership matched what the organization wanted. Make certain you review the presentation of your success stories and keep them top of mind for use in future tough interview sessions. Next, for your search attitude health, review your past successes as you regroup. Your career accomplishments, which could have been valuable for this organization, will be valuable for other superior opportunities. Shake off the initial disappointment and refocus on your Unique Brand Equity (UBE). Though you may not feel like it, immediately send your thank you letter with an acknowledgment that your sincere interest continues. Consider using a form of the Tee Letter (see Chapter 6, Ordinary Cover Letter Yips) in your thank you note assuring them your interest remains positive. Should the company elect to reconnect later, they will know that you were impressed by them and the discussions you shared. You will leave them knowing you are not timidly giving up. While not agreeing with their decision, you close the transaction on a very positive note. Your follow-up communication may result in a second shot and reconsideration for this or another opportunity.

What looked so certain but did not happen can be your incentive to move ahead with new resolve to move closer to the target. Realize the false front potential as you proceed with your search but accept how well you performed to get as far as you did in the process. Consider it an affirmation of your strong candidacy. Take those qualities that got you to finalist status and build on them for your next search encounter.

Chapter Twenty-Seven

Tighten Focus

Final Pitch Yips

Closer to the Goal, More Precision is Required

My analogical trip comparing golf to job search can help you get focused on planning and executing the "final shot" to your next position. When you are teeing off on a golf course, even though you know that there is a relatively wide target area ahead, there still is a chance for error. One's drive can wander widely off-target, even landing in the fairway of a neighboring hole. As long as it is not out of bounds or in a hazard, there is still a chance to recover for par. As we say, usually sympathetically, when a companion's tee shot sprays 30-plus yards off the fairway, "That'll work ... there's a lot of room out there." Closer to the green and the ultimate target, precision shot-making and taking dead aim at the pin become critically important. If you suffer from the yips, your pitch shot can fly over the green. Your putt for par can wind up ten feet past the hole. No one is happy as a par chance is turned into a double bogey or worse.

Let's relate the above golfing realities to search. You have had a long hard grind on the job search course. While closing in on your new employment goal, your last "short shots" may be the most difficult. You risk suffering from the "final pitch yips." You need to prepare very carefully to win the offer and negotiate that offer to your best advantage. Avoid egotistical or overconfident statements or actions that say, "I am the most highly qualified and valuable candidate you will ever find." On the other hand, don't project the "I-really-need-this-job" attitude. In stating your value to prospective employers, help them understand your realistic point of view and demonstrate a collaborative attitude that focuses on your ability to excel in their environment.

Depending on the situation and the people who are directing and determining the hiring decision, you must be armed with comprehensive knowledge of what they are looking for in a candidate. Once a fit with the firm appears near, you still have more to do to assure that the offer is acceptable to you. Check the list below for considerations you may find helpful in preparing for your negotiation process:

» Base salary, based upon researching reasonable market ranges

» Total compensation based upon the current value of your established Unique Brand Equity (UBE), not to be limited by your most recent base salary

» Relocation terms, based upon your family situation and the realities of your goals

» Starting date (a range of dates)

» Signing bonus (a possibility when you will incur loss of income or other inconveniences should you accept the offer)

» Incentive programs tied to performance

» Equity opportunity, as part of the career growth discussion

» Perks/vacation time, car, etc., usually predetermined but can be open

» Protection (what ifs)—terms of severance and outplacement policy. This is the only time to bring this up, consistent with your long term goals and your commitment to the opportunity

Some other guidelines for your consideration as you prepare for the negotiation:

- ✓ It helps to have a coach skilled in employment negotiation to provide objectivity and awareness of real-world priorities.
- ✓ Your requests must show how you will meet and exceed their needs.
- ✓ Be measured and realistic in your approach to negotiation. It is a process that requires care to develop mutual trust.
- ✓ The communication must show that what you have to offer, documented in your success stories, is based on answering their needs.
- ✓ The hiring authority must believe that you are the superior candidate, able to add value to their organization. Absent this convincing platform, your negotiation ability is limited.
- ✓ Do your homework. Learn what competitive salaries are for the job specs, the company, and the industry.
- ✓ Address why the employer should pay you more based on what you are bringing to the table, your UBE, your value to them.
- ✓ Keep in mind that discussing an offer requires collaboration with the other side of the equation. The total discussion needs to involve more than your base salary since that is only one measure of your value.
- ✓ Have one conversation on the multiple items you want to negotiate. You may damage your relationship with a prospective employer if you continue to bring up additional topics after the offer is made.
- ✓ Negotiate an offer only if you are prepared to accept it. If an employer goes to bat for you and perhaps increases

your package, it is very awkward at that point to decline the offer. Keep your reputation for honesty and integrity throughout the process.

✓ Think about what you want to negotiate and prioritize your list. This process is a give and take. For instance, if your package financial value is increased, you may be more flexible on your start date or relocation needs.

✓ Read the verbal cues. If it seems that an employer cannot negotiate more, back off and regroup. It is just as important how you express yourself as it is what you are asking for. Don't shut down the process prematurely.

✓ Finally, continue to count on your career coach, to keep your feet firmly on the ground with professional negotiation tactics.

The concluding phase of search is the most precarious. Care needs to be exercised so that the new employment does not start with ill-defined terms or unstated policies. Assure that a win–win feeling is shared by you and your new employer. Careful consideration and collaboration on important employment policies will provide a productive start for your new position. Remember, the closer you get to your employment goal, the greater the need to avoid the final pitch yips.

Chapter Twenty-Eight

Between the Ears Yips

Handling Rejection

Playing golf requires confident composure both physically and mentally. It is dramatic to view talented golfers who arrive at the green in regulation but end up with a double bogey or worse. Is it bad luck or what I call "between the ears yips"? Besides avoiding physical lapses, golfers must conquer the mental stress that can override their physical skill. Between the ears yips are common experiences for me and many of my golfing mates. Mental lapses start to show up before "the golf wheels come off." It may seem odd to connect prior unrelated or unfortunate events on the course to problems on holes that follow, but when an unexpectedly bad shot happens, it often has little to do with one's physical golf skill. Some professional golf announcers on television are able to diagnose yips even before the pro's precipitous nosedive.

"His focus was lost at the last hole when he missed the three-footer."

"That fan's camera click in his back swing and the resulting slice started his downward spiral."

"That misread putt got her to rush her next two putts."

"That last plugged lie on the lip of the bunker got inside his head and he barely made it to the green."

"The crowd's roaring response to Tiger's club selection rattled Sergio from 100 yards away."

Golf pros understand the between the ears yips, telling us that pressing to remedy a missed birdie opportunity or an errant shot may risk not being able to salvage even a bogie on the next hole. Indeed, trying to compensate for the last bad shot by trying to recover on the next hole can lead to a succession of negative events...the after-shock that stays in one's head and ruins composure. Similar negative "between the ears" events that occur in golf can and do happen in employment search. Being in search is difficult and debilitating owing to a wide variety of potential pitfalls. One bad event can put ego and psyche at risk. Imagine your elation when a wonderful job opportunity is identified. You are perfect for the position and you become one of the finalist candidates. A day later you are told, "You came in second although we really loved your terrific background and your responses in our interview." You may hear any of the following reasons for the rejection.

"We are going in a different direction despite your being a perfect fit for the position."

"You are very strong but you are overqualified for this position."

"We have decided to hire from within."

"Your background is superb but we believe you are not a precise fit for our organization's culture."

Recently, I worked with a client who, after the final selection round, was told he was "too New Yorky." Although his potential boss told him that he was the #1 candidate, the CEO felt he was overly confident and too forceful for his organization. Obviously, the final decision maker felt my tell-it-like-it-is client would not fit in a company looking for a "softer" executive, maybe one who would be more malleable. Good to know the rationale, but a difficult rejection from which to recover.

Events like these can deflate your search energy and ruin your campaign attitude. Our clients' experiences have shown that coming out of a horrible interview experience sets them back. It is important that rejection by a potential employer not overwhelm your psyche and begin a downward mental spiral. Just as in golf, loss of confidence can occur after a single bad event. While requiring some remedial work for the next interview, don't let that bad result attack your self-confidence. The successful job hunter needs to staunch the wound immediately. Bandage up, bounce back, and concentrate on taking the next employment "shot."

Sometimes, if studied objectively, rejection can lead to taking some needed corrective action. A review of the events should be mandatory. If unproductive techniques are identified, they can be dealt with. It may indicate that your Unique Brand Equity (UBE), was not communicated sufficiently to fit the situation and win over the competition. In your self-assessment, however, you may be too close to the issue to be objective in taking corrective measures. It will prove invaluable to work with a qualified career coach to get your campaign back on track.

No matter how you choose to handle the disappointment, the causes can be assessed, discussed, understood, and dealt with. Between the ears yips are difficult to conquer but with a realistic review of your campaign most mistakes will be less likely to be repeated.

Chapter Twenty-Nine

Tenacity

You're Still Away Yips

Closing in on the Ultimate Goal

PGA professional Mike Perpich offers superb advice: when you have a putter in your hands, "Watch the roll, not the hole." Applied to your search game, this advice will improve the probability of your success. On and around the green is where golf matches are usually won or lost. Those close-in shots will make the difference on the scorecard between par or better and bogie or worse. Watching the anguish on pros' faces after a missed six-foot putt, we realize how incredibly difficult putting can be, even for them. Unconscious yips, unintended movements, a sway, a jerk, a wobble, or a wrist flip will take the ball off its intended course. The mis-hit putt may leave the ball farther away from the cup than where it started. In golf etiquette, the person farthest away from the cup is usually the next to putt. When playing in a foursome and your first putt misses badly, you may cringe when you hear the frustrating comment "you're still away." A putt can be drained straight into the back of the cup if the read is correct, the direction is set, and the degree of "oomph" is adjusted to the slope and grain of the green. Combining all these elements in one stroke is what makes putting so difficult.

After settling on the chosen read of the green and the swing effort required, golfers need to trust their stroke and not focus prematurely on the end result. Mike adds, "You have to keep your head still and your eyes focused on the path you have chosen. If your head turns during your putting stroke, the club head may move and the ball will be drawn off the chosen path." Stressing out, trying too hard, can result in the "you're still away yips." This is analogous to the impatient career searcher who can't wait to hear the ball drop with a job offer. Like golfers, searchers should try to "watch the roll" rather than be fixated on the ultimate employment goal. Though the opportunity may be a perfect fit in your mind and seemingly so easy that it looks like a "gimmie," keep your campaign's focus on the sequence of steps that will get you on your path to the firm offer.

I remember being recruited many years ago for a top executive position. I felt I was fully qualified and obviously the chosen one. I believed that I had passed all the known interview milestones and interview levels so successfully that I began seriously and prematurely looking at real estate in the new location. On my third visit to headquarters I located a house that would be perfect for my family and I was more than ready to move forward. I did not keep my focus through to the final goal and the offer never materialized. I failed to watch the roll, and probably because of my impatience, I suffered the you're still away yips. That was a memorable early yips moments never to be repeated during the balance of my career—one I relate to my clients who look vulnerable to making that same error in their search.

What must be done to hear the sweet sound of the ball rattling in the bottom of the cup? Keeping your focus, preparing, practicing, and following your game plan will win the day. Watch the roll all the way to the offer that meets your career goal.

Chapter Thirty

Persistence

Repeat Performance Yips

The Second-Time Winner Challenge

In professional golf tournaments, according to past Masters Champion Nick Faldo, the most difficult challenge is to win the same tournament on the same course in consecutive years, (or ever). Repeating as a winner on the same course with a different field of competition and in a different frame of mind is nearly impossible unless you are of the Jack Nicklaus or Arnold Palmer caliber. Those who have done it are truly golfing giants. In the 2014 Masters Tournament we saw Bubba Watson win the event for a second consecutive time. It wasn't easy, as he was challenged and had to dig deeply to beat a young buck close to half his age. Repeating a professional golf tournament win isn't easy and neither is searching for a new job! I suggest that "repeat performance yips," the yips that make golfers unable to repeat a win, are similar to stressful situations in second or third job searches following past job hunting successes.

Many of our clients expect a smooth, uncomplicated search just like the last time, years before, when they were job hunting. When business growth was more certain, it was a searcher's market and much simpler and more unencumbered than now.

There were fewer competitors and, for those with strong personal connections, a job opportunity was easier to locate. A vibrant non-digital job posting system searched for talent more humanely, since the number of applicants was more manageable and the economy more positive. Career search today is challenging for millions in the U.S. who are unemployed, underemployed, or dissatisfied with current jobs. Because today's talent search is more impersonal and techno-centric, searchers must learn to use online communications and social media for communicating and networking. The conclusion is that your current foray into the new employment search arena may present a much greater degree of difficulty than the last time you were searching.

For those who have not been in search recently, below are several thoughts and alerts that highlight today's new search conditions.

1. In the past five years the number of qualified people in search, both unemployed and employed, has increased exponentially. Many are competent individuals with excellent educations, some with double degrees, who have contributed high value results to their firms and clients.

2. Ten years ago, recruiters were called into search and candidate sourcing engagements with regularity. Today, potential employers may choose not to involve a recruiter, even with a contingency agreement, thinking they can do it on their own and reduce the costs-in-hire.

3. Because it is so easy for today's searchers to use technology to build awareness of their candidacy, tens of thousands of hopeful candidates in the U.S. start searching daily. They send resumes to all known posting sites, recruiters, and potential employers. While highly inefficient, it is

tempting to use "saturation bombing" of resumes in an attempt to grab a job opportunity, any opportunity. Owing to less company loyalty, more fully employed candidates are taking the initiative to float resumes trying to find a new position. They hope their resume will be preferred over the resumes of the unemployed. The oversupply of candidates and their resumes results in slow responses and, unfortunately, resumes that never reach or resonate with potentially interested employers.

4. The low-growth economy and hiring budget uncertainties have added to employer vacillation and inertia in making hiring decisions. This situation is exacerbated by shaky confidence in governmental ability to get the economy moving in a positive direction. The lack of financial strength, health care costs, and regulation uncertainty creates further reluctance to make timely staffing decisions.

5. Often in the past, hiring decisions were based on gut feel rather than arduous searching efforts. I once received an offer for a position from a Fortune 500 CEO, saying of his decision, "I just like the cut of your jib." Today hiring assessments are less personal, more mechanical, and exceedingly bottom-line oriented. Stringent guidelines for HR staff usually state, "If you, or the scanner, can't verify all of the fifteen prerequisite boxes, don't send the resume up the line."

6. Biases have crept into the job search mix in recent years. The candidate's age can become an issue, as younger competitors with lower price tags are the competition. Advanced degrees are nearly mandatory today. Arbitrary demands like, "Don't bring me candidates who are out of work" and "I only want degreed candidates from these

ten universities" continue to be obstacles that were more rare in years past.

Considering all the obstacles, trying to repeat search success has become super challenging. My answer is to concentrate on fine-tuning your core competencies. Explicitly state your Unique Brand Equity (UBE) related to the job opportunity, and document how your individual involvement was pivotal in past career successes.

Bubba Watson could only equal Jordan Spieth's distance off the tee, so he fine-tuned his short game and green-reading ability to conquer the repeat performance yips and win the 2014 Masters Golf Tournament. Be inspired by Bubba and incorporate that ability to adjust to new competitive conditions to win the employment you target.

About the Author

C harles "Chuck" McConnell is Principal, Executive Managing Director of Stewart, Cooper & Coon-CT (SC&C-CT), Executive Placement and Recruiting. Chuck had been President/ COO when Stewart Cooper & Coon, Inc. (SC&C) expanded and gained national visibility in the career transition management marketplace. He has continued as a leading voice in career management services for over twenty years. Previous to SC&C, Chuck was President/CEO at First Career Corporation and FindCareer.com while serving as the online Career Expert for New York American Marketing Association. While serving as Executive Vice-President and Managing Director at BJKE/ Poppe Tyson Advertising in Boston, Chuck taught strategic marketing planning process at Emerson College. He has published numerous articles on career management and search preparation and has organized national and international conferences, assisting many to organize their career searches and gain traction for employment success. His published articles include "Resumes Say Volumes About You, Some Say It Better Than Others," "Tee It Up to Make Career Search More Productive," "Job Interviews Do Involve

Asking as Well as Answering Questions" and "It Takes More Than a College Degree to Move a Career Forward."

Prior to his successful work with transitioning executives, Chuck was the Senior Consulting Partner at The Watson Group, a strategic marketing communications agency based in Manhattan, New York. His career includes executive management positions with multinational marketers and advertising agencies in the apparel, consumer packaged goods, snack/confection, and toy industries. Chuck was President, Men's Sportswear at TAG, The Apparel Group Limited, building global acceptance of American-made branded apparel in over fifty countries. He has held officer-level positions at top-ten advertising agencies including WPP and D'Arcy, Masius, Benton & Bowles (DMB&B). While at DMB&B, as Executive Vice President and Assistant to the worldwide CEO he also directed the U.S. Treasury Olympic Support Account where he was awarded the American Marketing Association's EFFIE for Advertising and Marketing Effectiveness. His corporate success stories with major marketers include business building contributions for Kraft/General Foods, M&M Mars, Hanes, International Playtex, and Warnaco.

After graduating from DePauw University with a B.A. degree in economics plus a year at Exeter University in England, Chuck earned his MBA from Northwestern University's Kellogg School of Management. Though legally deferred, Chuck enlisted in Air Force Officer Training School where he earned Distinguished Military Graduate Status. He served during the Vietnam conflict with Strategic Air Command and PACAF, leaving with the rank of Captain, Management and Procedures Officer.

For twenty-five years Chuck has been playing golf. He has observed and dealt with the yips he and his fellow golfers suffer. While guiding individuals in career search, he has observed and chronicled the yips they share with golfers, both amateur and professional. Just as in golf, yips have to be conquered to become competitive on today's very tough employment course. Chuck hopes you will enjoy and benefit from the yips analogies he presents and gain leverage leading to your job transition success.